Charlotte Shand

Broken Child, Healed Woman

Broken Child, Healed Woman

Broken Child, Healed Woman

By Charlotte Shand

So You Can Write Publications, LLC

PO Box 80736

Milwaukee, WI 53208

www.sycwp.com

Copyright © 2023 Charlotte Shand

All rights reserved

No part of this book may be reproduced, or stored in a retrieval system, or transmitted in any form or by any means, electronic, mechanical, photocopying, recording, or otherwise, without express written permission of the publisher.

Publishing date: 5/15/2023

ISBN-13: 978-1-7376084-9-3 (sw)

Cover design by: www.sycwp.com

Printed in the United States of America

(Note: "The majority of quotations gathered by the author have been frequently in print and/or movie and television, as well as publicly accessible on the Internet; considered public domain. Where possible, the author and publisher have made their best efforts to credit any available sources for them. In the cases where it was uncertain where they first appeared, the information was cited as "unknown" or "anonymous." The information in this book is intended to uplift and inspire all who read it, or who have it read to them. The information quoted was kept as it was found and/or heard by the author, who makes no guarantee that the information one-hundred percent accurate, just that the author intended for it to be beneficial to all who reads it, or has it read to them."

Dedication

This book is dedicated to those who've never given up on me, even when I gave up on myself... My loving husband Lawrence Shand, who came into my life and showed me what true love looks like here on this earth... My oldest children, Deanna Smith, Dabreon Jefferson, Shelda Jefferson, who has never given up on me. They've stood by my side not because they had too, but because they love me and only want to see me win... My pastor Rodney Campbell, and my spiritual mother Rosezina Campbell, who never let me give up. The love, support, and guidance from these two have given me has been, and still is priceless. They've opened my eyes and heart to the fact that some people are truly God sent... And last but not least, my **BEST** friend Regina Fletcher, this young lady right here has been by my side, pushing me to be the best I could be. Always there with an ear to listen and a heart to help no matter what the need was. She is a true-life definition of a friend. There are many souls that crossed paths with me and in some way helped me, and for those of you know who you are, I thank you.

INTRODUCTION
(A child Lost)

Hello readers! My name is Charlotte Shand, and I am the writer of this book. This book will take you through the different stages of my life, highlighting pivotal moments since I was nine years of age. Bear witness with me as I take you down the roads of my life, and experience with me some of the trials and tribulations that have played a major role in me being lost, and then found.

The title of this book has massive meaning to me, *'Broken Child, Healed Woman'* because through this journey I've became lost. The child within me was force to be older and grown at times; and after this day I was never fully able to be a child again and this controlled my whole life. The repercussion from that day caused my life to slowly spiral out of control, and this did not just affect me, but also those around me, including my children.

Over time, I had to use every mistake, every heartache, and every unwanted act to help me regain what I've lost. The one thing I've found out during my journey is that, a relationship with God could change not only me, but also my atmosphere; and lead me to freedom from myself and freedom from others who've held me down. My childhood was ripped away from me at the age of nine, but through Jesus I begin to recover what was taken from me, what I have lost; and I was able to find that child lost and watch her become the woman God made her to be.

This is a true story about my life. There may be some situations that may disturb your spirit or may hurt your heart, but know as you continue to read I am alive and still pushing through. The only reason I am sharing this with the world is to be some help, to anyone who has been through or are going through similar situations. God gave me the strength to be a living testimony that He can and will deliver, make a way, and also restore. There is nothing my God cannot do.

The Beginning

My life ended as I knew it when I was nine years old.

"Knock, knock, knock.... Milwaukee police department, please open the door!" Is what I heard as I laid there with my heart beating so hard I thought it was going to come out of my chest. I knew we should have just stayed at grandma's house because she has sent the police. My sister and I slowly got dressed and got into the police car, both of us were scared. In my head I thought, *'we're in for it now, if she was mad enough to send the police we weren't going to be able to sit on our bottoms for a week. But wait, home is that way, where are we going? This is my uncle's house, and wait, everyone is here. OMG we're really in trouble now...'*

As we pulled up at my uncle's house it seems as if everyone was there, and they were all looking sad. I just wanted to yell out, *'we're okay don't be sad...,'* but the words wouldn't come out of my mouth, so I just stayed quiet as we walked up the stairs, passed everyone, and into the front room where our dad and uncle, and a few others were waiting. And again, everyone had sadness all over their faces. I felt like I was carrying a ton of weight on my back, it felt like every step I made took me minutes to complete as we walked into the house.

Once we entered the living-room we sat down on the sofa and waited for the worst punishment ever, but the room was so quiet, and in the mist of all my mother was nowhere to be seen. She wasn't even in the house, and then my dad begins to talk to my sister and I slowly, so slow that the words seem to fall out his mouth and stay in the air, "your mother is gone girls, I'm sorry."

"Gone?"

We both yelled gone? It was like someone took a hammer and hit me in the chest as hard as they could, and while I couldn't move or barely breath, my sister was flipping out. Shannon took out maybe four grown men that day and no one could hold her down. I just stood there waiting for the show to stop while fading away in the corner of the room, barely breathing and trying to figure out what we did to lose our mother. I was in shock, I wanted to yell and scream, jump and run, but I couldn't move; I cried but can't remember much but a numb feeling.

In my head I yelled and kicked and screamed but my body could not move. I was winded, and my chest was in pain from my heart trying to escape all of it. At that point, my life was over and my mother was gone; she would never come back again. One month before my birthday my mother was dead! Hurt turned into anger and then back to pain… *'why did she leave us? No good bye or I love you, nothing….'* For days and even years I had the same nightmare, me, my mom, and sister were walking on a bridge and my mother just walked off never looking back. This nightmare still wakes me up sometimes.

I often wonder, if the pain I had in my chest that night before the police came was due to my mom passing? Are we so connected that I actually felt her die? I had so many questions for God about that night I became motherless:

Why did my mom have to die?
Why didn't you make sure someone would take care of me?
And God, please tell me why did I lose everything at nine?
What did I do wrong?

The questions go on and on. As a matter of fact, the more information I received over the years about my mother's death caused me to have more questions, but I've learned to go on without answers. I used those unanswered question as tools to push me to live on in spite of. The day of the of funeral arrived and we all rode together, me, dad, and my sister. The silence was so painful; you could hear a grain of salt drop and the drive seem to be in slow motion. Once there, we were placed in the front (for the life of me I don't know why you would put two young children right in front of their dead mother) just to look at this big box that held my mom.

Once again, no tears but in my head, I was crying hard. We sat there through family members saying their goodbyes and the preacher giving his sermon, and then it was time for them to open the casket for the last time. I will ever see my mom again. As I walked up to the casket, I was even more confused because she looked nothing like my mom, what happen to her beautiful brown skin? And why did she have pink lipstick on? My mother would never do that, she had a natural beautiful clean face. This is not her; this can't be her and what did they do to my mom?! That day was long and confusing, and no one told me that a dead person's skin color changes in their appearance after they pass. And that's why the makeup must have been applied so heavily, I've learned that over the years.

The day ended with me and my sister being sent off because my dad thought it would be too much for us to go to the burial, so my sister and I never had the chance to say our last goodbye. For years, I didn't even know where my mother was buried, and still to this day no one in our family saw fit to put a head stone on her grave as if she was some unloved homeless person. Not the true helping person she was, like for helping my uncle over the years by putting him through school and helping him buy his first house. She deserved so much better than that. It still hurts to know that her wishes were not followed, she loved her children and would never leave us without.

Yet all the money she had for us was gone, our things were gone and we had nothing, and no one wanted us, but I will not get into that now. We shall walk down that lane later. This moment started a series of unfortunate, unbelievable, unhappy, and some of the most unreal events in my life. Yes, after my mom pasted my life took a horrific turn. I went from being a happy, spoiled, and loved little girl to a lonely, confused, and unwanted child with a 'hit me' target on my back with bad events and situations. Without any warning, my life as I knew it was buried with my mom that same day, and just like my mom, I didn't even get a chance to say goodbye to it.

I can honestly say, that sometimes just thinking about that moment still puts me in a distressed state, what I call my 911 moments... my forever painful days. As I got older, some of the memories from that day has faded away, but the pain stays stronger than ever, even though it has gotten me a little closer to God who I've found over the years. Well, He was never lost, let's just say who I've grown to know more of over the years. I never thought that I would ever be strong enough to get pass my mother's death and live because she was my world, and the fact that my family left my sister and I, to go through this alone and much more by ourselves, has put more logs on an already burning fire that had begun to eat away at our lives.

Yes, it's safe to say that some of the events that took place after my mom, still to me my beautiful Queen, had died could have been prevented if just one person, I mean one, would have stood up, in spite of how they felt. No matter what it would have costed them, because we were children and deserved a fighting chance, and given us a loving and safe home. Now, I know that life comes with its own shares of troubles no matter how you were raised, where you were raised, or with whom you were raised by. To have been able to start off with someone who loved and wanted to see us make it in life in spite of the raw hand we were dealt, would have made a world of difference.

I have forgiven my family for their very selfish ways and their endless excuses and reasons of why none of them could take the time out of their busy lives to make sure two small girls who've lost everything were taken care of and giving a chance at life. As my children say …IT'S ALL GOOD… because YOU REAP WHAT YOU SOW…. Now don't get me wrong, I don't wish nothing bad on any of them, (the younger me wanted them to lose everything and even die) but that was the hurt of being alone causing those thoughts. I didn't know how to work though my pain, it was like it crippled my mind and I could only think and plan out evil for them.

I wanted them to really feel what I was feeling. I justified thinking and talking that way by telling myself it would be the only way they will change, is to truly feel how my sister and I felt. Yet once again, (giving all thanks to God) I've learned that you reap what you sow, even for me and not just for those who hurt me, so I had to forgive them for my soul because is my testimony. I could not keep allowing them to take my life over and over again.

Needless to say, I have forgiven them and I still work on forgetting what they did so I can continue to heal from it. This is a long and worthy process that also helps me get a closer relationship with the most high. I am getting up there in my 40's and in no way, shape, form or fashion do I intent on carrying all that debilitating pain into another year with me. As a matter of fact, I believe that God allowed me to go through it all so that I can help someone else get through it. So, I ask you, the person reading this book, to please understand that this book is not just about the pain I went through, it's about me overcoming no matter the situation with God watching over me and covering me, I know sometimes he was carrying me.

The death of my mother was devastating to my sister and I, which was the start of many misfortunes down the road, but I pray you keep your eyes, mind, and heart open to the many wonderful works of God in my life as well. Know that there are going to be many rocky roads, and heart wrenching moments to come, but if you just keep your heart open, I promise you will see God do some of his best work in my life.

FLASH BACK… FLASH BACK… FLASH BACK

As a preteen there was nothing more exciting to me then dancing. I would pop, shake, and do the humpy dance all day. When I danced I was in a happy place, so it should come as no surprise that one of my favorite flash back memories was of me dancing. Yes child, I could remember it like it was yesterday. I was in a small dance crew of five, three girls and two boys, and let me tell you those boys could dance! I mean you put Heavy D's dancers and the dancers off the Luke videos together and you would have them. So, when they asked me to dance with them I was star struck on the serious side.

Look at me talking like I'm still in the 90's, I apologize but hey, the 90's had it going on…lol, showing my age for real. I've been watching them for a while and just thinking about how slick they were in the back of my mind, I was praying that one day I would be in a dance group like them. Well, I guess God was listening to me that day because they asked me and I was an official member and ready to show them all my moves. They put me and the girls to work immediately. We practiced all day and almost every day, whenever and wherever we could, we were getting ready for a talent show at MATC, which was and still is the community college of Milwaukee. I was so excited and surprisingly not nervous at all, I was to hype to be nervous and being in the group was the best thing that ever happened to.

I kept waiting for something bad to happen like someone to say, sike, this is all a dream, but no one did and I was really doing this. The day of the talent show came and it was a lot of people there; the auditorium was full and it standing only, not seats. Everyone was there to cheer on their peeps. We sat right in the front checking out the competition and then it was our turn, when they called our name my body went numb for a second, but once we got on that stage it was like I got super charged. It was my time to shine. I know I was up there with my group, but I didn't see no one, it was like all I seen was lights. We danced like our life depended on it, and the crowd loved it. They were cheering and yelling it was the BOMB… we won second place and left with a manager that day. I still get excited thinking about that day….

FLASH BACK… FLASH BACK… FLASH BACK

From friend to family and beyond

A few years later I was in Walgreens and I heard a familiar voice calling my name, for a moment I didn't recognize who this woman was that knew my name. At that time, I had been through hell and back, and for that split second, I was at a loss for words but it shortly came to me and wow, I was so excited it was my bestie's mom. I don't know if she knows how much seeing her and talking to her that day helped me. On that day it was like God knew that I needed to know that someone out there really did love and care about me. She and I talked for a bit about what was going on, I had to tell her that my mom passed and just like that she was gone and out of my life forever. That conversation is now somewhat of a mystery to me, I swear that after she left out the store I didn't remember much of what we talked about, but I do know that everything happens for a reason.

Reason #1 God had to show me that someone is out there that loves you and cares about you.
Reason #2 God needed to prepare her for the mission that he picked her to do.

Maybe, a year or two later I was staying with my dad and his girlfriend, and my step/half siblings' lives were kind of full of ups and downs. I didn't feel wanted in that house at all and it was like I was an outsider in my supposed to be own home. My step mother didn't want me there as much as I didn't want to be there, and my sister left me, and ran away by myself. My dad was busy with his own life, and as far as I can remember, him and my stepmother was always partying, having friends over, doing drugs and drinking. It wasn't that bad if they were together.

I got use to just being there and nobody bothered me except my little sister, who I swore hated me. She made it her business to get me into trouble, but as I look back at it now, what little sister, or brother didn't annoy their older siblings? So, just as I got use to my half-sister, big stepbrother and baby brother, my family was once again broken up. My stepmother decided that she wanted to give her life to Christ. She gave up drugs, drinking, partying etc. and my father decided he was content with his life and wished her fair well. I honestly don't remember if it went that smooth. Back then, still were the times where kids are to be heard and not seen, in other word grownups did their business behind closed doors.

All I remember was her packing up her and the kids and leaving. Leaving me there all by myself! The one good thing about that time was that my bestie, yes, the one and only, stayed two houses away from me. I was at her house every day, in the rain, sleet, snow, or shine I was there. It was almost like I had a normal family, I was able to go everywhere with them and since my father was caught up in his drug engulfed world, it never really mattered that I was at her house all the time. Even though I was at my bestie's house a lot, I still stayed with my dad, but because her mom basically took me in as if I was one of her own kids, I was able to eat there, sleep there, and even go to school from there sometimes.

That arrangement is what kept me from taking a bottle of pills and praying that I just died. I was able to be a kid and do kid things, but the fact that I had to go home kept me a little depressed and I never fully let go and enjoyed anything because I knew at the blink of an eye it could be all taken away from me. One thing I did do was learn how to make everyone laugh so they wouldn't focus on me. Yeah, I kept them laughing so they wouldn't see that I stayed in a dope house where my father sold drugs out the back room, or that it was very seldom that I had something to eat in the house, or that I had to stay locked up in my room to keep from being touch or harassed by the old nasty dope heads that stay coming and going at my house.

So yes, laughter worked well. It kept my life secret so I didn't have to feel anymore messed up then I already did. One day, my father decided that he could trust one of the men that was always at my house to watch over the house while he was gone. I was waking up to this very grown and very smelly man in my bed holding me down and grinding on me; I never got dressed so fasted in my life! It was early in the morning and all I could think of to do was run to my bestie's house, I've never been so scared before in my life. I thought he was going to follow me or try to stop me. My legs were shaking so much that I almost didn't make it to my bestie's house, but once there I told no one.

I was not ready to let the cat out of the bag about how I really had to live, so I just acted like it didn't happen. I wish I had not done that because it caused more problems for me in the long run then it would have if I would have just told, somebody. But knowing my dad, I would have sent him to jail if telling him because I know in my heart he would have killed that man, and then I wouldn't have had any parent left. I left it alone and stayed far away from that sick perverted half of a man. After that, I stayed more and more at my bestie's house so much that I barely went home. I was eating there, going to school from there, going to family outings etc. It was truly like a dream come true to be part of a real family again.

    I slowly became just one of the family. My bestie's mom treated me no different from her children she birthed. When she went shopping for them she went shopping for me; I was like one of her children because I even got in trouble if I did something wrong. I know that may sound funny me being excited to get punished, but to me it meant that she actually took the time to care about what I was, or wasn't doing. Unlike all the other adults in my life who sometimes didn't know I even existed. For that brief, and I mean real brief moment in my life I was happy. Yeah, there were a few hiccups but nothing worst then what I had already been through, so I thought.

    Until one day, I was home, at my bestie's house alone, for the life of me I cannot remember where everyone was, but I was in my little sister's bed sleep. Yeah, I was accepted by the family so now I had four sisters and a little brother, it was great, and all of sudden I felt someone shaking me and hear them saying, "come on, get up."

    I slowly opened my eyes and there he was gently pulling me up, I didn't understand what he wanted, or why he needed me to get up, but then it happened. He begins to touching me and not in a father daughter kind of way. I pushed him away as hard as I could but he was so strong, I begged and pleaded for him to stop but he just kept rubbing me and touching me in parts a grown man should never touch a little girl.

    I finally was able to break free and I ran to my sister's room in the back and hide in her closet. I was so scared, and I could hear him opening doors looking for me; I was crying, and at that point terrified. I sat still and quiet as possible. I even stop breathing for a moment, but he found me and then he grabbed me out of the closet and closed the room door and said, "don't act like you never done this before."

    Then, he begins to pull out his manhood and push my head towards it. Needless to say, that was the first time I ever seen a male private part.

Next thing I know, he stopped just like that. I don't recall what made him stop, but I know I was so shaken up that I ran to my dad's house as fast as I could. I laid on my bed with my door locked and in a daze. I just couldn't believe that the place I went to for safety now has also become a place I feared. As I think about it now, I can truly say that God was covering me and protecting me from that man, to have him just stopped in his very sick tracks by letting my head go and walking away. Yes, I believe it was God. In all, I still felt confused and alone wondering why were men so bad? And what have I done to make these two men believe that it was okay to try to take my innocence from me like I was nothing? I never came up with an answer for that question, and after a few days I decided to try going back to my bestie's house for two reasons:

Reason #1 I didn't want to explain to anyone, not my bestie or my father why I didn't want to go back. I felt that it would have caused more problems that I didn't need in my life and I didn't want to lose my bestie because she was my sister now, and her mom was my mom.
I guess in a little way I was being selfish. I just couldn't lose my family.

Reason #2 My father house was nowhere for a kid to be, there was always men and women there who were using drugs, and never no food. Sometimes, my father would just leave to handle business that put me in harm's way as well, I was just tired of being locked up in my room.

So, I came up with a plan to always stay around someone while I was at my bestie's house. Never did I sleep by myself, watch TV by myself, or nothing; and it worked for a while, and everything was back to normal. Life was full of us being kids again, yes!!! It seemed like, once again I made it through a rough patch and that I was going to make it, that is until he found other ways to touch me. Here we go again, this man will not stop. He would grab my breast or hit my butt as I walked by him. He always found a way to touch me somewhere somehow. I was constantly being sexually abused by that man and the only thing he never did or had a chance to do was rape me, thank God. Although, he did try once but again, God had prevented that from happening.

It was one night and all of us kids were laying in the living-room, I was on the floor and my sister was on the sofa, and he came in there just as bold as ever trying to get me up saying, "come, get up, come here."

Just to touch and groping all the while his own children were laying in the same room with me. It was like he was possessed or something. His eyes looked dead and I would not move, and eventually he gave up and left me alone, but little did I know my bestie heard and maybe even saw everything. After he left she woke me up and that wasn't hard do because I was faking sleep anyway hoping he did not come back. She was crying so hard I almost forgot what just happen to me because I was worried about her. She pulled me by the arm and we marched right into mom's room.

Now, by that time it hit me that she knows and I instantly became scared. Oh, no don't tell, she's going to kick me out thinking I betrayed her. Oh, no please don't be mad at me, was the only thing running through mind. Here is the woman that took me in and treated me like her own, and her husband won't leave me alone as if it must have been something I did, but to my surprise she believed me. She was so sorry, and as a matter of fact, she put him out. That night was so scary because I never saw a woman that mad at a man before. That one event in my life changed the whole structure of our relationship, we were no longer just besties but real-life sisters and God had blessed me with another mother.

Still to this day I feel as if she was, is, and will always be my angel here on earth. Over the years we had our ups and downs, but no matter what comes my way she will always be my mom and my angel. I even named my last-born child after her so her name can carry on. So now as I look back on all the times before my mother died that I spent at my bestie's home, with her mom and siblings, I was getting to know the family God had for me. The bond that my sister and I had with each other while we were young, carried on becoming so much more in a time when it was needed. I truly believe that once again, God was looking out for me. He knew the road I was going down and he put some escape routes in the mist for me. Oh, how I double heart, love God.

That night they all became my family. We became closer than ever, and lived as if I was blood. I had a mom again and she wasn't prefect, but she was loving, caring, and a bit strict, in all. She was the hardest working woman I knew. She did whatever she had to do for her kids and was not taking any shorts from no one, I often joke about how my mom was the real Medea. Just watching those Tyler Perry plays and movies be having me rolling, because I see my mom all over again. She really did not and will not play about her kids, or family; I thank God that he allowed her to cross my path and come together because even though it wasn't perfect, I don't know where I would have ended up had she not took me in.

Two houses

I was lucky I had two houses stayed where I pleased on any given day of week.
I was lucky I didn't have to run far when he touched me I hit two doors down or up and my getaway was complete.
I was lucky I didn't have to go far if we had no food I know her table always had a plate for me it was cool.
I was lucky I had two beds two bathrooms two kitchens and plenty of jogging shoes to get to each house. I never needed keys one bang on the door and it was open I guess GOD knew when I had to escape.
I guess I was lucky I had two houses I just wish one of them were safe.

Finally, the day I have been praying for came, one of them was gone and I didn't have to run no more; yes, my mom and my angel here on earth put him out and he was gone. It somehow didn't feel as good as I thought it would feel. I could finally walk around without being in fear that he would catch me alone while in bed and touch, grab or rub on me. Finish what he started. This was not a good feeling at all. Instead of being happy for myself I became sad for my sisters, who until I came alone had a two-parent household. They had a dad who was there in spite of what he was doing to me, he was there and I took that away from them. I felt so guilty about it. I just single handedly tore a family apart.

That day was truly one of my darkest days of my life. Just knowing that because of me a family, a family that I love I may add, was never going to be the same again. As they yelled and argued that day I became invisible in my mind and just stood there out of the way. It was as if I could not move or talk, hell, I couldn't even understand what was going on. I mean, did he really just risk his whole life to attempt to rape a child? I just wanted to ask him why he do it, why did he risk his marriage, his family, his freedom, why???? But I could not say a word. I was so scared and didn't know if he was going to lash out at me or try to hurt me, I just didn't know.

I replay that night over and over in my head often sometimes without even trying, but like a bad nightmare it pops up in my head, and still right now today I am still mad and confused about the whole situation. My heart goes out to my mom and sisters, and brother. Even though they don't show it much or talk about it like it never happened and I'm guessing that's how they were coping with it. I know it affected each one of them. It's funny how kids cope with pain. Everyone is different, and has his or her own way of dealing with things, by either burying it or facing it so they can live on. For me, coping with all the hurt in my life changed me into a chameleon. I never show how much pain I am in no matter what, I laugh it off and always became the life of the party. I truly laughed to keep from crying.

I wanted fit in so bad that I would change like Wisconsin weather to fit into any situation, you would never know if something was wrong with me unless I told you, but I did not do that much because I wanted to be a normal kid. All my friends were having normal childhood issues like, couldn't get the shoes they wanted, or couldn't go to a party, or they had to be in the house by eight o'clock sharp and things like that. While on the flip side of things I was too busy dealing with molestation, semi homelessness, a mom who committed suicide, a dad who was using and selling drugs, and biological family members on both sides that didn't want me. No one came to see if Charlotte was okay, not one person from my mother's side or my father's side during that time in my life came to check on me. If they would have, they would have seen that there was no food in the house and my dad had turned the back room of the house into a smoke room while I was going from house to house just to feel safe. Which ultimately resulting into me breaking up a whole family.

I get furious just thinking about the destruction the selfishness of my family caused in my life. I will never understand how the death of my mom could bring out the worst in those who were close to me when she was alive. I remember being around them all, but it was like they all passed on when she did because I didn't hear from them or see them, my mother's brothers were in Milwaukee but I only seen them a few times while the chapter was playing out in my life. I guess everyone went on with their businesses and families. The fact that their nine and twelve-year-old nieces just lost their mom, and their dad was on drugs while selling drugs living the fast life. That didn't matter to them because we were not their problem, so me becoming a chameleon was imperative to my survival.

I couldn't go on showing pain and weakness, I did not want to be an outcast or victim, I just wanted to be NORMAL… but I learned that I was far from normal. It's funny how God allows you to go through things young while He is actually preparing you for your latter. I read in the Bible that we are a peculiar people, we are not of this world and He has set us aside to do his will.

1 Peter 2:9 King James Version (KJV)
[9] But ye are a chosen generation, a royal priesthood, an holy nation, a peculiar people; that ye should shew forth the praises of him who hath called you out of darkness into his marvelous light;

As a child I didn't know what being a peculiar person was, this revelation came to me years later while in my late 20's. At this point in my childhood life I was still just trying to hang on to reality and keep my sanity, what little bit I had left. It's sad to say that I thought about killing myself more than once or twice, hell, let's face it, I thought about different ways to end my life every day. I mean, who would care? My dad was basically caught up in his own life, my mom committed suicide under the pressures of this cruel world. Let's not to forget that I had just broke up the only thing in my life that was remotely normal, my new family; yeah, my life was definitely not getting any better at that point.

    I was at the point where I had to put on my big girl pants and move on, yeah at the ripe old age of thirteen I had to learn the hard way that life isn't fair. Thirteen is often said to be an unlucky number and it was life changing for me it was unlucky and hurtful and painful and just downright confusing yes one may say that my life was starting to resemble one of those lifetime movies it just kept getting bad every time I thought that things were getting better along came a storm and each storm came with more fire then the last one.

    Sometimes it seemed that I was born to be in pain, that I was put on this earth to go through it, but somehow, I found some good in life. I don't know if I just got use to nothing good happening in my life or if I just got numb to the pain or both, but somehow, I just started living no matter what I just kept living not looking for a way out any more. No more suicidal thoughts, at least then, and no more fear. I just kind of went with the flow of things, hell, I didn't have to see my abuser any more. He did not really come back to the house at that time because the wound he caused in everyone lives was still fresh and my dad was just not worried about me coming home every day. I was in my new home for good; sleeping there, eating there and even going to school from living there. That was the first time since my mom passed that I felt like living.

Why are you here

To build me up make me strong and fearless
Is that the reason you are here?

To be my friend make sure I am never alone
Is that the reason you're here?

As an angel to watch over me in the darkness
Is that the reason you're here?

Well my friend you're a GOD sent a true light in the darkness
And no matter the reason I am so glad you're here!!

That summer I met a person who right now is still my friend my good friend my family. She is my besties cousin and from the moment we meant we clicked like we were friends all our life. Now you put that in the equation with finally feeling safe and free and I had what you would call a win, win situation lol. (Although this is my life story for the privacy of everyone I have changed the names)

When Lena would come over we had so much fun just doing normal things like walking to the park to check on the boys playing basketball, or walking to the restaurant ten blocks away for ice cream. We enjoyed being around each other and I felt like I could tell her anything and talk to her about anything. Sure, I had my sister/ bestie to talk to but somethings I felt a little more comfortable talking to Lena about, somethings and still this day I don't know why because me and her were like day and night.

Lena had two parents that were still together, and she was giving attention and love by both, they did things as a family and were able and willing to give her the world where is I was made to fit into someone else's family due to no one in mine wanted or had time for me. I didn't know what it was like to have everything I needed or wanted after mom passed, but while she was alive I had that life that Lena had minus the two-parent home but when me and her started to hang out that life was just a fading member too painful to remember or even talk about. Somehow Lena brought it out of me I was able to share those good times with her and laugh and joke about them as well. It's like she brought out the goofy side of me and I never wanted to hide again as a matter of fact that's why I always find a way to laugh in the face of pain.

I believe that it is true that God place certain people at different times in your life some are for a season and only there to carry out a specific mission in your life and others are ROOTS and they are there for life. I still don't know if Lena is for a season or one of my roots so far, she is looking like a root to me. she and I had so many first together and mad fun we seem to always find something to do or talk about the weekends she came over were like gold to me not being gay at all but she was my crush lol. She reminded me, in a way of my life with my mom, we were so much alike but at the same time so different. Where I was loud and out there she was quiet and shy, but somehow, we had a good time in whatever we did even sneaking and doing stuff we knew we would get skinned for like sneaking over boys' houses and meeting them at the park.

But most of all sneaking over boys' house. I must admit I kind of talked her into the sneaking over boy's house, but she was down as well. There we were running around the neighborhood like Thelma and Louise getting into nothing, but it seemed so fun. Lena honestly was what I needed in my life, she was someone that didn't judge me or make fun of my living situation, she never treated me like an outcast like some people did on the low. She always, and still right now to this day encourage me to do and be better; she always made me feel like I had a chance to live the life I wanted to live and most of all she made me feel that I really deserved it.

You girl is and still is an awesome friend, now we never really had disagreements or fights but we have had moments when our lives didn't allow us to see or talk to each other much. When we got back in touch it was like we never left each other's sides; to me that is a friendship and real family. Oh, I have so many crazy stories I could share about me and Lena, stories that would make you cry from laughing so much, and stories that would make you cry due to the love, caring, and understanding that we always had and still have no matter what, but I will just leave you with this.

Some people say that you only get one soulmate and they use that in terms of a relationship between female and male, but I say if you're lucky or blessed you will have an opportunity to meet your friend mate, what is a friend mate you ask? A friend mate is a male/female that gets you like no one else, accepts all your flaws and love you anyway, that will listen to you without being judgmental, a person who is the same always no matter the situation, and most of all she/he encourage you and stands by you. That is just what Lena has been all these years, and I thank God for allowing her to be in my life.

Secret Shame

In the summer you would have found us girls hanging out with the 34th street guys because they were like the coolest guys ever. You would usually find us on our front porch or over one of their houses kicking with them, we all had our pick of which one we liked, but for the most part we all just hung out. One day they came over just to hang out, we had our boom box on the porch listening to the greatest hits from one of our favorite singing group New Edition, and oh, my God they blew us away because they song just like New Edition. It was like being at a concert in the front roll.

The one who song lead was everyone's favorite because he sounded just like Ralph Tresvant, the lead singer of the New Edition group, but the funny thing is he looked like Michael Jackson. Boy was he fine; soft spoken and everything. We use to try to get them to sing all the time, in between us doing others things which consist of talking loud saying nothing, playing tag, and yes, we even played hide go seek. Okay, it was hide go get it. This mean if you were found by a boy they get to touch, hug or kiss you. I think I was the bomb at that game. I put my tomboy ways to action, I would hide and if you found me you better knew how to run because I was out. It was all in good fun.

We spent a lot of time walking to the store, burger king, the basketball court, and back and forward to each other's house. I know it sounds boring, but we had a ball. Every time we all were together it was fun. Someone always did something to keep the laughs going, or sometimes we coupled up and chilled. No matter what we did or where we were, when those streetlights came on we all were at our own house. One day I had to go on 34th street by myself, I left my school belt over MJ's house the day before while hanging out with the crew. It was too late to go back to get my belt that day, now remember, when the street lights come on you better be home. So, I went over there after school to get the belt before I went home.

I had to hurry, we didn't have cell phones back then and my mom knew exactly what time we all made it home. I made it to his house rung the bell and his mom let me in. His room was in the back, I knocked and enter said, "hey, do you know where my belt is?"

He looked around and found it and said, "here."

As I grabbed the belt he pulled it back smiling. I told to come on now I have to go, but he just kept on playing pulling it and then grabbing me. Now, I was kind of mad so I pushed him and said dude stop playing I have to go. That boy looked me in my eyes, then closed and locked his door. I was beyond mad now. I pushed him saying stop I have to go, and he turned his music up and begin to pull down my pants.

When he was done, he gave me my belt, unlocked his door, smiled and hugged me like what just happen was what we both wanted. That boy took my everything that day. I went home and took some pills I don't know what they were, but I knew I didn't want to wake up. I never told anyone but my sister it was our secret and my shame. I felt that it was my fault I shouldn't have went there by myself, I should have stayed on the porch. Over the years I would see him and even talked to him. I guess I just let it go as a terrible mistake and forgave him. It surprised me how easy I was able to forgive him for raping me, but at the time I didn't really forgave him I just let it go.

I was grown and didn't care to bring up something that I, along with other events I keep buried for my sanity, but when I saw him it hurt like hell that he smiled and asked how my sisters were. He pretty much acted like it never happened, I mean I didn't expect him to run to me apologizing for something that happened years ago, but deep within I did want him to at least acknowledge he was wrong. Rape is a crime that takes everything from a person. It consumes your whole self being, makes you feel as if you are to blame, even dirty for letting it happen to you. I questioned myself for years why you didn't fight back? Did you want him to do that? I would ask myself. I walked around with shame written all over my face, but no one ever knew, life just kept going and I buried it just like I buried so many other hurtful acts that took place to me behind closed doors.

That day just confirmed what I was feeling about myself for so long, that I was nothing, a no body and the only way I would survive was to just smile and keep it moving. I often had dreams about that day and what I could have done different, but at the end of each dream it always ended up the same way. I was raped, so for months I was repeatedly being raped in my head. I finally stopped thinking about it and realized it was done and there was nothing I could do about it; I buried it so I could live with myself. Needless to say, I was still trapped because I never dealt with it at all. I had to accept it and then pray on it so I was able to really forgive and live. Once I opened my heart to God through prayer and I was able to truly forgive, and by forgiving my heart became lighter.

I begin to be free. No longer bonded by what he did to me that was his burden to bare, not mine. Thank you, Jesus, as crazy as it may sound it felt good to forgive. As my early years rolled by slowly I would find myself in between houses again, why? You ask; because the Child Protective Service, (CPS) thought they knew what was best for me so they begin to give my mom a hard time about me being there. I would never forget the social worker they sent to our house, oh, I hated her. I know you're not supposed to hate but I was young and she was the enemy that made it her business to take me from my home. This woman gave my mom the business for taking me in and keeping me out of harm's way.

She checked the home over and over again and she made it very hard for my mom, who was just trying to help me for free. Yes, I came with a check for about $740 or so, but she never asked my dad for anything because she worked two jobs and took care of me like she birthed me. That wasn't good enough for CPS, from her first visit I was on pins and needles because I knew in my heart that her mission was to take me out of my mom's home. From that time on I had it very rough; first, I went back with my dad for a moment, who by this time had moved to my granny's house. I was turning sixteen.

I still remember my sweet sixteen basement house party, oh, it was all that and a bag of chips. Yeah, I'm old. That was one of my favorite memories of course, it didn't go smooth. My big sister beat someone up for calling me out my name, then a select few got to come up in the house and we finished the party there with a cake fight, yeah, we had a ball. The party was over and it was time to get back to life, or should I say school because that was one thing my dad didn't play with, you were going your butt to school. So, he put me in the school that my big sister and my big cousin went to, North Division.

Now, I was a little tiny something when I went to that high school and it seem like I had a target on my back. Every female wanted to fight me, I just wanted to skip school every day but was scared of getting caught. I rather fight ten jealous females then get my butt tore off by my dad, so I went to school and dodged the ladies well. I became a pro with staying away from the haters. Life was cool until I met the boy that would become my first child's father. This boy was something out of a movie to me, he was light skinned, he was rocking a long jerry curl, and just a little bit taller than me. He also was a smooth talker. I was floored; the boy was everything I needed... because he liked me.

He gave me a lot of attention and talked himself right into my pants, which was easy to do sadly to say. Up until that point in my life every man that I had any contact with either took from me or tried to take from me. I had been molested by those who I looked up too, those who were supposed to be my friends, those who I didn't know well, but they felt like they had a right to take from me. So, when my soon to be child's father came a long I was already hurt, used, busted and confused. I honestly thought that was all I was good for being some man's sex toy. Before my first child's father no man or boy showed me anything other than lustful attention, so the attention I received from him took me over. He was my world. I didn't do anything without him even though I was constantly fighting other girls over him, and if I wasn't at home everyone knew I was at his house.

I was with him so much that we were kind of a package deal, if you see him you seen me, then it happened, sex; I gave up my goodies and became pregnant the first time. I wanted to be happy so bad, but it was the scariest time in my life. What was my dad going to say? Or most of all what was he going to do to me, how was I going to take care of this kid, and of course, is he going to leave me? I was on a roller coaster that turned crazy and there was no turning back now. I just had to put on my big girl panties and tell my dad.

I believe I was a few months when I told my dad and surprisingly, he was calm when he told me to get an abortion. He said, "I didn't want you to drop out of school like most girls do."

I ensured my dad that I would finish school and he dropped it just like that. There was no tension between my dad and I, which seemed kind of strange to me, but on the flip side it was great I could enjoy the fact that me and the love of my life were going to be parents soon. I often thought about what kind of mother I was going to be, but most of all I thought about where was baby and I going to stay truth be told. I was not in any better of a living situation, the house was full with uncles, cousins, my dad, and oh, yeah, the roaches which took over the house.

It was like some kind of takeover because they were falling from the ceiling, in the refrigerator, in the sink, on the dishes, and sometimes in the bed. It was not the right place to have a baby, so little by little I got back to my mom house and by that time she had moved to a whole house, and she took me back in with open arms. I was ecstatic that I was going to be able to have my baby in a clean house with my mom who I needed because I was only sixteen and knew nothing about taking care of a baby. The joy of being home only lasted for a little while, though by the time I turned about four months here come CPS again putting their nose where it doesn't belong with that same sad song.

"Since you are not a blood relative of Charlotte, we have to remove her until this can be resolved with the courts."

Really? I was in shock for all those months that I was with my dad, and let's just put it on the line here, the house was disgusting and filled with roaches. Once again, dope usage was in the air and no one from CPS came to check on me, NO ONE! Not even that fat smelly social worker who made it her business to take me out of the only household where I was eating and not around drug users and sellers. I was pissed at this time and didn't want to cooperate, but I was only sixteen so I had to.

CPS put me in a home with teens who were gang banging, who were being pimped out by their own mother, and even with one who watched her sister blow her brains out playing Russian roulette. For the life of me I didn't understand why I had to be punished because my dad couldn't pass a drug test, or because they didn't want me to stay with someone who actually wanted me and not the check that came with me. She wanted me. I was so miserable in that home it was like jail to me and I hated it so much. The highlights of being there was we got to cook with the caregiver and I loved to cook, we baked cakes and cookies, and talked and laughed. Plus, being able to speak to my mom and sisters on the phone kept me going while I was there.

I remember one day, in the morning we all were getting ready for school, as I walked down the stairs the carpet was loose and I slipped and fell down the stairs. Now mind you I am pregnant; I got up and was in so much pain I had to lay back down. I was in some real bad pain and felt like I was going to lose my baby, so I laid down in the bed. Once I was able to move I went back down stairs and told the caregiver who instead of taking me to the hospital, told me that because I missed school I had to stay in my room all day. I was so confused? I asked her, "how is it my fault that I slipped on the stairs and got hurt?"

This woman gave me a look that she didn't understand why I was mad and told me to go back to my room. I was upset for having to even be there because the adults in my life can't get their lives right. I am not sure how long I stayed there, but I was still pregnant when I left and finally I was able to live with my mom without anyone coming to take me away, or so I thought. I quickly learned that as long as CPS was in my life I was never going to be free to stay with my mom. Hell, they took me out of her home every chance they had.

First, they put me with one of my mother's brothers and his longtime girlfriend. I still loved her and their children. Everything was alright for a bit, but my little cousin had a terrible crush on me it was funny. I guess when your young you don't care about family you just know you like that person. That was a little stressful because he would go in my room and touch my things. One time he took my darkest lipstick and ruined a picture of me and one of my friends from school, and no one did anything to him. That was just one of the things he did, but he never got in trouble for anything. School time rolled around and every month my uncle was receiving a check for $740 for me being there, now this check was to take care of me and my needs but this man gave me $150 and told me to buy my school clothes, supplies and anything else I needed.

Personal hygiene products etc. while him and his girlfriend would go and get their kids school shoes, clothes, and supplies. I remember that they would have this big truck full of school supplies, but I couldn't use any of it. It made no since how he felt that he had the right to take the $740 check, that was meant to take care of me and only give me $150 a month. He took the rest which was about $590.00 to do God knows what with it, and once again no social worker came to see if I was okay while I was there. No pop ups, no calls, or no visits period. I even told the worker when I went into the office about my uncle's drug usage and selling, but still no one came, but they made me stay so I left.

I ran away if that's what you want to call it. Well, I call it escaping and I ran right to my mom's house. I was about fifteen years old at that time, but the social worker from hell found me again and off to my dad's house I went and there I ended up pregnant at sixteen.

Now rewind back to a little before I was sixteen pregnant, and back in my mom's house. The world was good again but because of the risk being taken I was always on pins and needles. I could never really let my guard down because every time I did in the past, I was taken out of the home and had to be ready to run pregnant and all. I was ready to go, I kept a bag packed on the low just in case I had to hit it. Thank God I was able to give birth to my daughter while living at my mother's house. Man, she was perfect; just as red as she could be and fat. The first time I saw her I was in love real love, that I would die for you love.

I just wanted to give her the world, because I was at my mom house at that time she was getting my checks and I was able to do for my little papoose. My baby and I were happy, but that wouldn't last long. One day the social workers came to remove me again, yes, again and took me back to my uncle's house where he kept all my money and often treated me like a stepchild. Things started out okay at first because they were so happy with my baby they acted like she was theirs, but under all the happiness for my baby he was still only giving me $150 a month to do what I had to do for me and my baby. It was so hard living there but once again no social worker visits at all.

The final straw was when I was accused of stealing money from my uncle. He swore up and down that I took his money, never once did he look at his kids, no he only looked at me. I was so pissed because here I am, struggling with the little bit of money you give me and not causing any issues for you while you and your family living off what the state gives you to take care of me.

Then to top that off, you accuse me of stealing from you? Please, I was done and I hit it so fast out of that house. I ended up staying with my baby daddy and his mom for some months and even then, my uncle would still only give me $150 and tell me that the money is for where I live. I told him I don't live in your house anymore so I need my money. This man had the nerve to tell me he doesn't want no one to take advantage of me, lol. That was so asinine for him to say when he was the only one that was taking advantage of me and the money the state was giving to take care of me.

He never gave me anything when I was with my baby daddy, I would call him and say I need my money for pampers, food, and rent. He would never give me no more than $150, and the killing part about that was he never saved up the money for me. He spent it all on his kids and his home. So, there I was homeless and penny less with a baby because the state said I had to live with a blood relative. Now at that point in my life, nothing was going well; my baby daddy was involved in criminal activity, and cheating on me. I had to get out, it was just too much for me to handle, but I had nowhere to go so I stayed.

While I stayed with him he would go out and visit other females and then come home like everything was fine until one night, we went to a party, one of those good old house basement parties at his aunt's house. Little did I know, he was cheating on me with the girl who stayed upstairs from his aunt. A big fight broke out because of that and he ended up shooting someone in the butt. Now there I was with a baby at his aunt's house while he is running, and boy did I feel so dumb. His sister and I finally got home and I was in shock, there I was living with my baby daddy while he is out cheating on me at his aunt's house. I'm caught up in some bull because he couldn't keep his thang in his pants, but I stayed; and the next night his mom and I, and the baby got in her van with her boyfriend and they took him to Chicago to his dad's house to hide out. He cried so hard on that trip because he was forced to leave his baby because he messed up.

After, the ordeal I seized the opportunity to leave and moved back in with my mother, whose door was always opened to me no matter how many times I was forced to leave when I showed up on her door. She greeted me with open arms like I never left. Once there, it was back to normal; I had chores, curfew, school, etc., life was somewhat normal again. My mom got me back into school and I was busting straight A's, and loving it, no more having to live off $150. My mom was finally able to get the check for me and she would just cash it and give it to me, but I would never take it all. I believe that check was giving to take care of me and where I stay, so I give her some of it for herself and the rest for me. I was a kid and she actually took care of me, I didn't need the money and she didn't just shop for her kids, she shopped for me too, so I felt it was only right to give some of the check and use the rest for my baby.

It was so hurtful to me how a person who was/is of no blood relation took care of me without that check, and then also, still took awesome care of me with the check. It's safe to say money didn't change her at all and my own blood relatives took that check and did for themselves and not me. They did the bare minimum for me which puts me in the mind of this bible verse:

1 Timothy 6:10 King James Version (KJV)
[10] For the love of money is the root of all evil: which while some coveted after, they have erred from the faith, and pierced themselves through with many sorrows.

Because with all my heart I believe that they were evil to treat a child like I was nothing and only take me in their home for a check; and once they got the check they did wrong with it and only thought about themselves. I could go on and on and on about that matter, but I won't, there is no need for me to get upset all over again about that. Why? Because God has truly been good to me even when people were not, He's always been good. I know what you want to ask, why did God let them do that to you? I feel like we all have to go through struggles sometimes but it doesn't mean God is not there along the way, suffering is one of the fruits of the spirit and no one know how long it will be or when it will take place. I do know that I did not go through any of it for nothing. Hopefully, there is someone who is reading this book that need to know that you can make it and that God is there even when it doesn't feel like he's there, but He's there.

Galatians 5:22-23 King James Version (KJV)
[22] But the fruit of the Spirit is love, joy, peace, longsuffering, gentleness, goodness, faith,
[23] Meekness, temperance: against such there is no law.

     Here is the fruit of the spirits, this is something that I didn't know when I was young, and when going through situations no one gave me a bible or taught me anything in the word but God was still covering me. So, when I got of age and started wanting to know more about God those verses played a good part in my understanding of why my life was what it was. There are so many verses that helped me and still help me to understand and live today. I wish I had this knowledge of the word when I was young but then again, I don't know what God's plan was for my life; everything I went through good, bad, and ugly may help save another soul who is at the end of their rope and thinking about giving up.
     As I write down some of what I had to conquer and go through brings up so many mixed emotions, but one thing for sure, I would never be able to get over it until I could be real about it. With God I got over it which brings me to one of my favorite verses:

Philippians 4:13 King James Version (KJV)
[13] I can do all things through Christ which strengtheneth me.

     I can do all thing's verse helped me get over some of the hurt from my early years. It seems like it is harder to just forgive and forget those who wronged me in my early years. I had to stay in prayer asking God to help me heal and forgive. I believe it was so hard because in my early years I was a young child, so those who done me wrong were sick; they had to be to do a child like they did with a clear conscious. One thing that my early years did was make me over protective of my children as they were growing up. I would do whatever for my kids because I was their mom and friend. I had my babies young, so I grow up with them. Having my second baby at eighteen pushed me right into adulthood.

I was ready to get into my own house and be an adult. I had two children and did not want to put my mom through having to raise more children because I was hard headed. I had two babies at the same time my little sister had three, and she was ready to move out on her own as well. My mom helped us get ready and gave us the speech… take care of my grandbabies or I will blah blah blah, they were not good words she expressed to us. Just as quick as that conversation was done so was my childhood. No more being moved by CPS, no more having someone taking all my money, no more no more no more…. yes, my childhood was over and at that time I was so over it.

Never again did I want to return to it. Some people often think about what they would change about their childhood if they could, I wouldn't change anything because I refuse to ever go back, it is what it is. No need to go back. I am reminded of a song the praise and worship team sung at my church, Crossing Jordan Ministries it's called, *'Moving Forward,'* the lyrics of that song is spiritual motivation for my soul. I could listen to that song all day every day and never get tired of it. It gave me life, as the young people would say.

"I'm not going back, I'm moving ahead, I'm here to declare to you my past is over in you, all things are made new surrendered my life to Christ, I'm moving… moving forward. What a moment you have bought me, to such a freedom I found in you you're the healer that makes all things new, yeah… yeah… yeah…"

I want to truly thank Hezekiah Walker for making this song, when the praise and worship team sings this song I am bought to tears and to my knees in thanks. This song truly confirms that I should let go of the past once and for all and focus on my future in GOD. The first time I heard that song Minister Rosezina, from Crossing Jordan Ministries in Milwaukee, WI was singing it. Not singing it, but singing it to my heart. This was around the time in my life when I realized I had to really start forgiving and moving on, or I was never going to truly be able to live in God's will; with all that in my soul. I was in my mid 30's and headed straight for destruction, or as the seasoned saints would say, '...to hell with gasoline underpants on,' but let me start from the beginning, or shall I say middle? So, you can get the full story that started with the ending of my childhood.

FLASH BACK... FLASH BACK... FLASH BACK...

I was about fourteen when the most embarrassing, yet funniest thing happened to me. It was so funny that it was talked about for years; such a good laugh, but embarrassing as ever, lol. There I was, along with the 37th street crew, which was my sister and our friends who stayed on the corner house on our block, we were chilling inside their house like we normally do. With her brother and cousin all coupled up listening to music, I was with her cousin and he was my first real boyfriend; I was crazy about him. He was tall, dark, skinny with this black, silky curly hair, he was fine, and he had this thing where he would repeat everything when he talked. Almost like a light stutter, it was so cute; and he was a little bit older than me, which really made him look good to me. Not pervert old, just a few years older.

Well, on this day I guess he had convinced his self it was the day that we were going to take it to the next level and I was a still a virgin at that time. You know, go all the way, and this he decided without me lol, but any who moving along, our friend's house was like a mansion that had three floors. The second floor was where her parent's bedroom was, across from the girls' room and on the third floor was the boys' room. There we sat on the third floor hugged up and kissing a little while listening to music when like out of nowhere the lights were turned off, now I don't know what anyone else was doing, but all that was in my head was… GETTING OUT AND HOME AS QUICK AS POSSIBLE. As he hugged me and got closers I was planning the greatest escape of my life.

He went to feel under my shirt and I jumped up like I was on fire. I screamed that I had to go to the bathroom and took flight down the stairs. I was going so fast that I don't even think I touched all the stairs with my feet, lol. Once I reached the first floor I ran out the door and two houses down to my house and up the stairs like the police was chasing me. I did not stop running until I was in the bathroom at my house. Everyone including my friend's parents called me the great escape artist anyway, lol. Yeah, I was the joke of the hood for a while, but we stayed together, and he spoiled me rotten; and of course, we had some good laughs off that day.

FLASH BACK... FLASH BACK... FLASH BACK...

The Rolling Years

Childhood had dropped me like a bad habit once I became a two-time mom at eighteen, no I wasn't put out or forced to move, as a matter of fact my mom wasn't even angry with me, more disappointed with me because of all the mishaps I had already encountered as a child. She did not want me to rush into adulthood because I never had much of a childhood. I guess she wanted me to be able to know what love was and not to be easy prey for one of those no-good brothers that was out there just waiting on a broken chic like myself. What she did not know is that I had already falling prey to my twins' father who was training to be a pimp/drug dealer, but we'll talk about that later.

Here I was eighteen on my way to nineteen with two children living with my mom, my sister who was right behind me in age but had three children at that time. I was practicing how we were going to ask our mom if we could move out, see my mom was and still is the type of person who you had to come at correct. She wants to know how, when, where, and with who, before she even thought about the answer or the question for that matter. When we asked for permission to move to our own apartments, to our surprise she said yes, but not without a threat. In her loud raspy voice with the vein going down the side of her neck she let us know that we better take care of her grandbabies or else…and we know what the or else meant.

Low key, I so wish I would have waited to move out, regret was written all over that decision. I was definitely in no way shape, form, or fashion ready for the world I stepped into with rose color glasses on. I suddenly learned what an abusive relationship looked and felt like. Especially, when you don't have momma to run to, or in the next room to stop the madness from happening. Yes, I was in my first abusive relationship. Now I have been in two not so good relationships, but none of them did me any bodily harm, or put me in positions where bodily harm or even death could have been done to me.

I was in teenage relationships, my only worries were being cheated on or lied to nothing I couldn't handle, but this relationship took me through a whole another world that took me deeper and deeper into the danger zone. By this time in life, I seriously thought that I had seen the worst and that nothing could be worst then being molested, raped, homeless, and motherless, but I was so wrong. As matter of fact, I had never been more wrong in my whole entire life. What this man had for me was not just sick, but down right criminal activity and I had no way out. Sure, my mom said she would be coming over to check on us, but she never came to check on me, only my sister. My house could have been full of chaos and she would have never known it because she never came, but she was always at my sister's house.

    I know what you thinking, but no my sister stayed right next door to me, we both stayed in apartment #2, in two buildings right next to each other. Everyone close to us knew I was basically on my own. I had no one to just drop by and check on me, so I learned how to live life sadly to say. Sometimes life lived me and wore me out, but back to this man who had me wrapped around his whole hand. I met him before I moved out of my mom's house, and the first night we met we talked the whole night; no touching at all, we just laid on his mattress talking about everything. MC Smooth was getting his mack on and it blow me away because he was nothing like he looked.

    Well, you be the judge… he had a long perm, tall, dark skinned, well dressed, and such a smooth talker. I thought for sure I was going to have to fight him off that night, but no, he was the perfect gentlemen. Who knew almost two years later he would be my boyfriend, slash pimp, slash daddy, slash abuser. I was deep in over my head, but no one knew or cared he didn't stay with me, but he came and went whenever he please; and he hit me whenever he please as well. That was normally when he didn't get his way. I had to be the perfect little girlfriend or else doors were kicked in, braids pulled out and eyes blacken etc.

    Now I can honestly say that this wasn't all the time. He was more of a talker then a hitter, but he didn't take any shorts at all and I just learned how to stay out of harm's way. One thing I had going for myself is that I had my own house and wasn't living with him, so I had room to breathe, room to do me, and at that time I had room to take up the family business which was of course selling drugs. Yes, I felt like it was an easy hustle by watching certain family members, and because I seen a few family members do it and get away with it I tried it. Besides, I needed money. That once a month check wasn't enough and as I said before I had no help.

    I know that was still no reason to risk me or my children lives, but nothing was going to stop me. I had to do what I had to do and at that point that was what I had to do, so I became a mini drug dealer selling crack cocaine. I learned how to cook it, chop it, bag it, weigh it, and sell it. I would go to one apartment to cook it and back to my apartment to bag it up and sell it. Although, it may look glamorous on the television and in the movies, it was far from it…. miles, waves, leaps, and jumps from glamorous. I was always paranoid at the beginning, and it was terrible every time someone knocked on the door I was shook, my nerves were worst then a ninety-year old lady who've been mugged. I had this recurrent nightmare that I was going to open the door and the police would be there with their guns out screaming, "…get down and put your hands on your head this is a raid…"

Then, I would wake up in a cold sweat looking out the windows and doors like I was smoking my own supply. That nightmare went away but then a new one came. In this nightmare I was being robbed and raped while my kids were in the same room, and just before the man grabbed my baby girl I woke up. Again, running to the windows and making sure all the doors were locked while sweating like I just came out of a storm. You would think that would be enough to stop me, the constant nightmares, waking up in cold sweats, fearing me and my children lives, but once I started it was like I couldn't stop. I was a nineteen-year-old mom of two with enough money to do what I wanted when I wanted it and it was a good feeling. I had steady customers coming with money, household items, and even food.

It was like I was living in a movie, and the best part my man didn't know anything; it was all good until I had a customer bring me some baby clothes. It was some nice stuff, guess jeans and other name brand items. She begged me to just take them because she had no money and she needed a hit bad. I never seen anyone like that. I was at a loss for words, she looked like she was going to pass out, tears were in her eyes, her clothes were dirty, her teeth looked like they had dinner from two nights ago on them. She was bad. So, I took the baby clothes and the radio she had and gave her two dimes of crack before closing my window, and I felt like I just stabbed myself in the heart.

How could you take baby clothes? What is that little baby going to wear Charlotte? Why, what kind of person are you? This is what I was saying to myself and I don't know if there was answered back. I tried so hard to justified what I was doing, but nothing I said worked. I couldn't convince myself that it was right to take from another child and take advantage of the fact that the mother has a drug addict and kept on feeding her the problem. I was taking from her child, an innocent baby. It became hard for me to even look at myself in the mirror. I called myself setting ground rules that I wouldn't break so I could keep selling without my conscience eating away at me.

Rules:
1. Accept only money.
2. If no money only household items instead.
3. No baby clothes, toys, etc.
4. Only take IOU's from regular customers.

    I put rules together thinking that it would help me to keep doing it without hurting anyone when in actuality, I was hurting someone every time I sold a bag of death. I was hurting the person using and their family especially, their children. I had slowly allowed myself to become everything I was pissed off at my dad for being. At that point I was no better than him, no better than anyone who sold drugs, we all were single handedly killing people off. One would think that would be enough for me to stop.

    Then, I had my come to Jesus moment, so I should have stopped instantly, but not me, the girl that always had to push everything to the limit, yes, I kept going putting out more and more product and doing a great job at hiding it from my boo. It was like I lived a normal life, just a regular mom of two with a boyfriend that comes by every now and then, nothing out of the ordinary besides the fact I'm selling dope out my front window. As I look back, now I see how blessed I am to be sitting here writing this book today because I could have been killed or in jail just now getting out. But God covered me even when I didn't know Him, He protected my children and me, He covered us all. It brings me to this verse:

Romans 2:11 King James Version (KJV)
[11] For there is no respect of persons with God.

    Because at that time in my life I was not living a holy life, I was so wrapped up in the world I didn't give God a thought. I knew not of Him, but He knew of me and what He had planned for me and who He needed me to reach, so He covered me even in my not so good decisions I made.

PRIASE BREAK.... I CAN'T THINK ABOUT WHERE I COULD HAVE BEEN IF HE DIDN'T LOVE ME ENOUGH TO COVER ME KEEP AND PROTECT ME... I JUST HAVE TO SAY THANK YOU JESUS!!!!

I'm back. Sometimes you just need to drop whatever you're doing and give God some praise because it could have been you. I have seen some of the people I sold drugs to over the years, some have cleaned themselves up and some has slowly been killed from their addiction. I still feel that hurt in my heart that I played a part in destroying their lives. I also thank God for forgiving me from all my wrong doing to those and their family. I know some may say it was their choice but let's be real, drug addiction is a disease that takes over the mind and the ability for them to make good decisions. Now I am definitely not justifying someone using drugs in no way, form or fashion, just putting this out there for those who are going through it with love ones or friends who are dealing with drug addiction.

I'm owning up to the role I had in their lives, I sold it to them and that makes me just as guilty as they are for using, may God continue to have mercy on my soul. I never really got over being that type of person. I have done far worst things in my life, but I think it will take a little more time for me to get over that. To forgive myself is so hard, but in time I will, I know my God has already forgiven me once I confessed my sins and repented. He forgave me.

1 John 1:9 King James Version (KJV)
⁹ If we confess our sins, he is faithful and just to forgive us [our] sins, and to cleanse us from all unrighteousness.

Acts 3:19 King James Version (KJV)
¹⁹ Repent ye therefore, and be converted, that your sins may be blotted out, when the times of refreshing shall come from the presence of the Lord.

I not only asked for forgiveness, but I stopped selling drugs because I couldn't go on living in fear of feeling depression from seeing those people every day willing to give you everything they own for one bag of death. That changed my views on selling drugs for good. I managed to stop without any incident, thank God. My boyfriend was still in the dark, my mom didn't know anything, and my children were safe from harm. I wish I could tell you that was the last time I made a decision that put me and mine in danger, but I would be lying out the side of my neck. Let's just say I never went down that street again and move on, because it's about to get really hot up in here and I'm not talking about the weather.

The hell storm that I speak of came in a form of a tall, dark, and what I thought was a lovely man, but who was every bit of a lying conniving snake on a mission to mode me into his next victim. This was a ride I was not prepared for at all, no one could had ever made me believe that he would put me through the hell that he put me through, this man had me believing that he would never hurt me, use me, or abuse me like all the rest have. He was different, he talked to me and was opened to me about himself, and for once in my life I was able to be close to a man without him pursuing me sexually. He made me feel like a woman, a beautiful woman with the world at her feet.

The way he talked to me in the beginning was like it was me and him against the world, and I was the perfect Bonnie to his Clyde. No man had ever talked to me that way and no man had ever made me feel the way he did, I guess it was because I was so use to men using me for their own sexual gratification. They were focused on getting it from me voluntarily or by force, but this one didn't talk about that subject or even attempt to persuade or seduce me into giving it to him at all. With him, it was my choice, so I thought. Now that I look back, it was his game because he was a pimp and he made the woman feel as if they had made the choice to do what he wanted, but when back on planet earth if they decided not to carry out his wishes they regretted it badly.

As our relationship moved forward he became more demanding and controlling, he had to approve on what I wore, where I went, who I was with, and even who knew where I lived. It begins to interfere in my relationships with my family and I had to keep them at a distance, I mean it wasn't like anyone was close to me anyway. I didn't get visits from anyone, if I wanted to see my family I had to go next door to my sister's house where everyone visited, so hiding what was really going on in my relationship was fairly easy, but not a good ideal. I can recall one day he just showed up at my door and he was heated. We argued for a while and next thing I know my braids are pull out my head and I took off running out that door.

I ran so fast but he was right behind me with those long legs. I made it to the hallway of my sister's apartment building yelling and screaming, and just in the nick of time my sister opened her door with the phone in her hand and he just stopped and looked at me, then walked away. My heart was beating heavily and I could barely breathe, and my whole body had just collapsed on the stairs. The funny thing is, my mom was on the phone, I guess he heard my sister saying, "mom, he over here fighting Charlotte..." and he stopped. I was confused on how could you have that much fear or respect for my mom but still try to beat the hell out of me.

It was kind of like being in the twilight zone, or like having an out of body experience. I could see myself running from him, watching as he got closer and closer to catching me. God was truly covering me that day. I still don't recall what I did to tick him off that day because I normally try to stay on his good side. (you know, be a good girl for daddy) My whole mission was survival, I didn't know what all he was capable of and I for sure didn't want to find out, so I did whatever he said and that was it. Life was sweet, he was happy I was happy, until he was ready to go forward with his other plans he had for me. To my surprise this man was grooming me to one of his girls, (a street walker, prostitute) I was in disbelief.

I knew he was a small-time pimp/dope dealer, but I just didn't think that for real, he would expect me to sell myself for him, and by the time I'd came to term with what was really going on I couldn't stop it because I feared stopping. So, there I was in boot camp learning how to sell myself to the highest bidder, and scared to death that someone was going to get me alone and kill me or hurt me really bad, but what was I to do? He found me whenever I so called ran and he promised me that no matter where I was he would find me. The killing part of it all is that, I was in love with him, so some of what I did was not out of fear but from I have to make him happy. Up to this point in my life I did not have a healthy relationship with any man, not even my father who played a key role in why I fell for that man.

The relationship we had was a mess, he ordered me and even went with me on the bus to find men to sleep with for money, that was the lowest part of my life. After, that night I begin to hate myself and I started to wish God would just let me die, but something also happened that night as we were on our way back and he couldn't really look me in my eyes it was like he was sad or something. I couldn't place what was wrong… I did what you wanted me to do what? After, we got off the bus and walked back to his house silence filled the air, and I was a ball of emotions and I didn't know what to expect.

This was my first time doing this and I had worrisome questions, did I get enough money? Did I take too long? What? I was so scared. Morning came too quick for me and I wanted to lay down all day but that wasn't happening because I had to get home to my babies. So, I got up, got dress, kissed him goodbye, and walked out the door still a little shook up from last night, but so thankful I wasn't killed or hurt and that I was on my way home to see my babies.

As I walked home, I made up my mind that I would rather die than to put my life in danger like that again, I just couldn't believe that I did that. I felt nasty and so unclean, I remember thinking, how can I face my babies knowing what I did, how could I even face myself? Here I am, after getting away from all those years of sexual abuse, from those sick minded men. Why would I go and disgrace myself for a man? I cried that whole day. I couldn't get over it… I sold my self for what, a man! I made up my mind I was done with him. I locked my door and didn't come out my house nor did I answer my phone, I was on the ran without leaving my house.

Me and my kids stayed locked up for days and I felt so free laying with my babies watching TV just enjoying my gifts from God. For the first time since my mommy passed away I had peace. No one knew what I was going through, it was just me, my kids, and peace. It was a week before I had contact with him or anyone. Again, I think the shame of what I'd done kept me in hiding, it was like, everyone knew when in reality no one knew. I felt like I was in one of those moments on TV where everyone was pointing and laughing, and calling me sluts and hoes, but then I would open my eyes and no one was saying anything.

Who knew how much one night, one action would affect my sanity. I had to struggle to keep it together and didn't want anyone to know. I thought about just taking a bottle of pills but I couldn't just leave my children like that, who would take care of them, love them, raise them? NO ONE, so that was out. At this point, I pulled my chameleon costume out the closet of my life and went back to fitting in, that was the only way I was going to make it. Just act like everyone else, make them laugh with your little jokes that really come from your life. It's cool, they will never know, hell, no one paid that much attention to you anyway, so yes, I went back to my childhood mind and pretended that I actually had a family that loved me.

I was worth as much as my sisters, but deep down, well, not even deep down that stuff was on the surface and we knew that I was nothing like them at all. I didn't have anyone who gave two pennies about me, and everyone always say, "Charlotte good, she got this." Really, what Charlotte were they talking about? Because this Charlotte was not fine. I was dying inside, walking around my sisters who had it all wishing I could have just had a piece of what they had. I was sick of feeling like the black sheep, but sadly, it would never stop and only get worst. The jealousy I had for my sisters was turning me into a not so nice person and I became that B word to everyone. I kept a frown on my face and talked down to people, I acted as if everyone owed me something, but my man at the time got a little glance at who I was turning into and he kind of liked it.

I guess that's when I truly became Bonnie to his Clyde. He never put me on the street to sell my body again, but he still treated me like I was his property and I better did what he said, which I did. Well, sometimes, and other times I did what I wanted or said what I wanted, and take whatever he dished out. Yes, I was broken. I didn't care what he did to me along as my babies were alright. I had no value anymore, he would slapped and kick me around, made me have sex with his friend, and when the black eyes or bruises were visible, he would kidnap and hide me in his dope house until all marks were gone. It went on like that for a while and I said nothing for many reasons, here are four of the most important ones:

1. I feared that he would kill me if I told anyone.

2. I didn't want my kids to ever know what I was going through.

3. My family on my father side was kind of crazy and I knew it wouldn't end well.

4. I didn't want my family to kill him.

As strange as it may sound I was in love with him, from what I had learned about what love over my eighteen years on this earth, this seem like love. He fed me, brought me things, gave me money, and sometimes he would say he loved me. So, I kept my mouth closed about what I went through in my relationship, it wasn't hard to do since no one ever checked up on me. My mother nor my father ever came to my house so I was living in a perfect little storm. I would often just look out the window and wish I was some of the people I see walking by not even knowing what their home life was like. Yet, I had this notion that no one on earth life was bad as mine so window shopping gave me hope that I will live a normal life one day.

      I prayed that it would come before my man finally killed me one day. I wanted to really sit down and talk to someone and express how I really felt about this relationship I was stuck in, but at that time it seems like everyone was having issues with their relationships. We were all dealing with cheating, physical and verbal abuse. It was like it was something in the water. These boys in men bodies had lost their mind and we had to find ours, so we could get away from these unhealthy relationships. Needless to say, I kept the real hurt inside because I never felt that it mattered what I was going through, maybe I was wrong, but I could only go off how I've lived. Again, why if you love me you never came to check up on me or called me just to see how I was doing mom? I never got over that I had people but only sometimes, but I got by.

Help

I been used, abused, beat on, and left for dead.
Every man that touched me made sure that my soul was dead; and all I could do was allow the issues of my pain through tears to pour out alone on my bed.

Help

I cried but no one heard me, I yelled but the noise of this world drowned out my tears.
The pain from a constant beat down took a toll on my body and the loneliness only makes it worst; no one sees, no one cares while this man is taking his time to make sure I'm dead.

Help

As I pour out all my fears alone on my bed,
I would have cried help but you all were too busy, I would have screamed help but he took it and the scream was no longer in me. So now all I have is the pain in my head, I will just let it all pour out on my bed.

Well, needless to say, my relationship was still going strong. I was still going to his house or he was over my house, and for a while things were good. We were going out, talking, and all that others stuff couples do until one day the peace was shattered. I was on the phone with my big sister while he was there, and for some reason he just didn't want me talking to her so he asked me to get off the phone and I said no. Then, out of nowhere he slapped the phone out my hand and it hit the floor. I looked like, why, what did I do? Not even ten minutes later there was a loud knock at my door, and as I opened it there was my sister, her boyfriend, and my child's God dad pushing their way into my apartment.

It was like a movie! They had guns and they were pissed that I couldn't move or say anything. They begin to whoop his butt and left him with a message to never touch me again. Of course, the police were called but he didn't press charges. He told the police that if she was my sister I would have done the same thang. My head was spinning. He looked so bad that I cried and cried, I never wanted that to happen, but I couldn't take it back. He left that night and we didn't talk for about a week. I had mixed feeling about the whole ordeal:

1. I felt like he got what he deserved.

2. But then I felt like no one deserves what he got.

3. I still loved him and hoped maybe he learned his lesson and we will be better.

My mind was playing out so many different scenarios our relationship could end up, but only time would tell and that time was short about a week and a half. He called me and asked me to come to his house. For some dump reason I wasn't scared at all, but I did ask was he mad at me, and just trying to get pay back. He said no. He wanted to see me and apologize to me. I was shocked and in disbelief, but like a love-sick puppy I went and I was so hurt looking at him. I also forgot about the black eye I wore, or the hair pulled out all over the floor. I was only thinking about how he had knots on his face and bruises on his cheeks.

I was so sorry I just cried in his arms, and then we talked and made up, and it was like we were the only two people in the world that night. He told me things about him I would have never known and after that night, we became closing than ever.

Until one day months down the line. I was shot while in his house, and I remember like it was yesterday. I was sitting in the chair in the living room right in front of the window and he was sitting on a chair on my right facing the wall. We were talking and I kept asking him for something to eat, finally he said, "okay, I'll make you some noodles."

Soon as he got to the kitchen the first bullet went through the wall where he was sitting, and here I am in front of the window scared. So, I jumped up to run to the bedroom and was shot in my leg; all I felt was a bad string, the numbness, and then I fell. The police came and I was taken to the hospital, where they cleaned my leg where the bullet went in but it didn't come out. I was able to go back home that night but that's when the pain kicked in, thank God for pain medicine. I was in shock because I've never been shot before and it was unreal, yet the most bizarre thing from the whole incident was there were about 120 or so bullets holes in the back of the house where we were.

None went through the window I was sitting in front of so if I would have never moved I wouldn't have been shot, but on the flip side, if he would have never got up to get me something to eat he would have been shot right in the forehead. All I say when I think back on that night is look at GOD, that could have been the end of my life, but God. For years that shooting hunted me and him due to my family insisting that he shot me, even though there were over 120 bullet holes in the house and one of the bullets gazed the top of the baby's crib upstairs. We still ended up together and had two beautiful baby twins, until he went to prison and I'm happy to say that ended the chapter of that part of my life.

Me and him kept in contact while he was incarcerated, but I went on with my life I had now four children and was a single mother it was hard, but it was so peaceful not having to watch what I said, or did it was just me and my babies. It was a little piece of heaven for me, my children had my full attention and I also could be free to be me, know me, and love me without looking over my shoulders. I had a taste of freedom and I loved it. I guess the relationship was not a complete bust and I had learned some interesting things about myself that helped me grow into the woman I am today.

Taken

I left you for a moment, safe and sound; I never thought in a million years
that my actions would cause you any harm. No, not my sweet little peanut
my heart beats for you. No one knows how much of my world was lost, when like a thief in the middle of the night they took you all with no cause. Leaving me alone to mourn what should never had happen, they just snatched you all and now my life is on pause. I couldn't eat, I couldn't sleep, my God I could barely breathe; the loss of my blessings would surely be the death of me.

The day started off just like any other day at home, I was sleep on the sofa and my children were on a big pallet on the floor right next to me; the twins were in their chairs and cartoons was playing on the TV. I got up, fed the babies with my oldest girl helping. She was so in love with her little brother, she would hold him all day long if I let her, she was my big helper. So, we fed and burped them and got them ready for their wash up when I noticed that the trashed needed to go out and the clothes needed to be washed. A mother's job is never over, there's always something to do or redo, lol. So, I changed the pace, instead of washing the twins up I put them down for a nap in their chairs on the floor and I told my big girl to watch them while I run down stairs.

I took my big boy with me because he was only two, and still not feeling the two new ones that suddenly took his place as the baby so I kept him close to me. Before I walked out the door I took one last look back, babies sleeping, big girl watching TV okay, and I walked out the door. First, I throw the trash away, then I put the clothes in the washer, and we headed back upstairs. Soon as I opened the door my big girl had a look on her face like she was so scared. After that, everything went in slow motion. I grabbed my baby boy and started yelling... "what did you do baby what did you do?" Without an answer I called 911 as quick as I could and just held my little man so tight, he was trying to cry so hard but he was barely making a sound. I didn't understand what was happening to him, "Jesus help me," I cried.

The ambulance came speeding down my dead-end street, I heard them and opened the door crying, "please help me, please help me," and honestly, everything went blank. The next thing I remember is being in the hospital watching them put tube after tube in my baby and I just cried, and then they pushed me into this room where my family was and begin to tell me how my baby had a 50% chance to live. His brain was swelling and they had to stop it. I was in shock, I couldn't speak, I couldn't think, I couldn't hear, I could see their mouths moving but couldn't hear what was coming out.

"Why is this happening to my baby?" I yelled. It seemed like the walls were closing in and everyone was against me. I finally got a chance to talk to my big girl and she was so scared but brave at the same time. She told me, "mom he was crying so I picked him up but he wiggled out my hands and fell on his car seat. So, I picked him back up but he fell again, mom I'm so sorry he was crying." I hugged my big girl so hard and kissed her, and then I told her it was okay they were going to make our baby all better.

I wish that would have been just what they were going to do but it was so far from the truth. We were all moved into a bigger room because there were some many of us, and then it begin. My older sister took my children home with her and my dad, mom, and other sisters were still there at the hospital with me as we sat and waited for more information on how my little peanut was doing. A man and woman entered the room and asked to speak to me in private, they took me to a room with one table and a few chairs inside and begin to ask me about my life, and about my family. These people were bringing up things that happen to me years ago when I became pregnant with my first child.

I was confused and pissed off at that moment. They had kicked me out of the room with my baby and weren't giving us any update on how he was doing. On top of all that, now they want to play twenty-one questions. No, I was not with it, so I started asking the questions like how is my baby's wellbeing and when can I see him? As I waited for the answers to my question the male who I found out was a detective begin to ask me what happen to my son? So, I told him what my baby girl told me (because I know she was telling the truth) and as I finished speaking he begin to ask me did I hurt my baby and did I ever want to harm my children?

This man even asked me did my dad want me to have an abortion when I was pregnant with my first child, and do I know who hurt my baby and am I scared to say so? I was becoming upset by the second. I looked at that man, and again told him what happened with tears rolling down my face, I went over every detail of that day; before, during, and after my baby got hurt, and it still wasn't enough. After the last time I told them what happened the detective advised me that until this was cleared up they would have to keep my children in protective custody, I was not allowed to be in the present of my children unsupervised. He said that I will be contacted to appear at court and as he walked out he asked did I have any more questions?

I was at a loss for words. I was crying out of control and while I was talking to them the police had went to my sister's house and took my children from her. By the time I went back to the waiting room with the rest of my family my sister had called my dad crying and yelling that they took my kids. The sadness on everyone's face was unbearable and

I suddenly felt like the walls were closing in on me once again. Within ten to fifteen minutes I'd lost the only things that mattered to me the most, my children and they were gone because of an accident, an accident, God why? I kept my house clean, my children were clean, fed, and loved. I had a house, they had beds, clothes, and most of all love. I just didn't understand how they could take my babies from me, but they did.

The same system that was taking me from my mom and putting me in group homes and homes with relatives that didn't want me, now had my children. The Milwaukee police/detectives had the nerve to take my four-year-old daughter down town and record her telling them what happen treating my baby like she was a criminal. They also went to my house and inspected it like they were looking for drugs or something, but at the end of the day they found out that everything my daughter said was the truth and that I was not a child abuser and that I would never hurt anyone of my babies. But the sad thing was, since CPS had already started a case against me they would not give me my children back.

I was continually being harassed by the police, they watched everything I did, and even showed up to the hospital while I visited my baby boy. One day me and a friend of mine went to see my baby boy once he was out of the ICU, and I was able to hold him. I was so excited to see him, so we stopped and got something to eat first and then we went to the hospital. When we made it there we stopped in his room first, I gave him a kiss and then went down the hall to a family waiting room to eat. I was so happy my baby was smiling and he looked so good like nothing ever happened, then it happened. The door opens and in walked two detectives suited and booted with funny looks on their faces, both trying to make small talk.

Me, so young and naïve, I was twenty-one years old just sitting there joining in on their useless small talk. After maybe fifteen to twenty minutes went by, the real reason they were there came out.

"Ms. Jefferson, we just have a few more question for you concerning your baby's condition," one of the detectives asked.

"Sure," I said. he said

"Do you mind if we go down town to the police station? I'll get your friend a ride home."

Again, "sure," I said. I was so dumb.

So, we all walked out together and they lead me to a paddy wagon, opened the back door and helped me in. The ride was fast because before I knew it we were there. The door opened and one of them helped me out, but I could tell the mood had changed. One of them told me because we were walking into the station he needed to put handcuffs on me, pat me down and be finger printed, along with my photo being taken; so basically, I was booked. Now I was pissed and confused, and PISSED AT THESE GOOD FOR NOTHING DETECTIVES for tricking me. I'm in a room full of criminals, eating thick as a brick, bologna and salami sandwiches. I couldn't cry, I had to act strong even though I wanted to roll up in a ball and cry like a baby so I just waited; I even had small conversations with some of the ladies around me.

Then my name was called and one of the detectives was waiting for me to take me to his office. I see now what he was doing, trying to make me feel comfortable and get on my good side so maybe, just maybe I would confess to something I didn't do. I walked in and had a seat on the sofa in front of his desk while he sat in the chair in front of me. I must admit I was livid by now; this man had tricked me into cutting my visit short with my son to bring me down town and put me in holding cells with criminals and now he wants to talk! But I was cool, and I answered his questions in detail over and over, and over again.

"Did you hurt you son?"

"Did you drop your son?"

"Did you shake your son?"

"Can you tell me what happen to your son?"

"Where were you when it happened?"

I answered those questions so much I sounded like a broken record. My mouth was dry and my throat was sore, and I just wanted to sleep, but this man just kept on asking me questions. At one point, he reminded me of my mom the way the vein in his neck had popped out and he was getting redder by the minute, but my answers were still the same.

"I did not hurt my baby and I would never hurt my baby…" I got so mad that I yelled at him, *"I didn't hurt my baby, if I didn't want him I could have just had an abortion. Why carry them eight months to hurt them it doesn't make sense?"*

Silence filled the room. I could tell by the look on his face that he was madder than a pit bull in a dog fight, but no way was that man going to get me to confess to hurting my son. That just did not happen, not never; it was an accident that's all. After what seem liked forever he was done, and instead of saying I was free to go he took me to another holding cell, but this time it was the big one. I was called to take a shower and put on my jail uniform, and then I was led to a pod; I was given this heavy mattress which was really nothing but a matt that I had to drag to my room. I couldn't believe it… I'm in jail! It really didn't kick in until it was time to eat; oh, my goodness, the food was tasteless, but the so-called red Kool-Aid was the best part of the meal

Then gym, and right before bed time my name was called, "yes?" I'm out of here is what I was thinking, but due to the experience that I'd been having with the police and CPS, I knew all too well I wasn't going home yet. I got up and walked slowly to the front of the room and the officer said the DA wants to speak to me. So, they put me in cuffs and walked me over to the DA's office; soon as I walked into his office I could tell he was upset. I just begin to pray that he wasn't upset with me as I sat down; he introduced himself to me and explained who he was, and why he wanted to talk to me.

From my understanding, he was saying he didn't know why I was booked and in jail at all. He asked me to go over what happen and what caused my baby to be admitted into the hospital. Again, I told him what happened that day, like I told everyone else, word for word including every detail, from the moment we woke up, to me taking my two-year-old son with me to take out the trash. Not forgetting to mention, throwing in a load of clothes into the wash, and then coming back up to see something wrong with my baby. He asked questions in between me telling him what happen, I think he was trying to use that method to try to trip me up, but I was telling the truth so that tactic didn't work on me.

Finally, after I told him what happen about three times and answered more than thirty of his questions, he looked me into my eyes and said, "I don't know why you are in here. I am sorry, we will get you out of here soon as possible."

I was stunned and happy all at once. He believes me. Finally, someone believed me. My release process started immediately; they had me gather up my things and an officer walked me down to change back into my street clothes. I was issued a bus ticket and let me go. I ran to the nearest bus stop and went to my mom's house. I couldn't go back to my house I just couldn't. From that point on I was homeless from my mom's house to my friend's house, going back to my house without my kids was just too hard.

Without You

Without you I could never go on, without you my life is nothing but a sad love song.
Without you what am I here for, without you life is not worth living anymore.
Without you my love, my blessing, my life is no more than a hand full of tears that needs to be healed.
Without you I can't move, I can't sleep, without you I don't even want to live.
Without you my heart forgot how to love, without you my whole body is forever numb.
Without you my world is always down and my life refuses to go on, you're my everything, my blessing and my reason to live. That's why without you I'm nothing and can't do anything, for with you is the only reason why I can live.

Eventually, months went by and I was going to court. Through a court order I participating in parenting classes, going to psychiatrist appointments, and being able to have supervise visits with my children. But I was still dying inside. They had me doing so much, I call it jumping through hoops just for them to let me visit my kids was ridiculous. The fact that they proved it was an accident and I didn't hurt my baby at all should have been enough for them to let my babies come home with me, but no. I was a young black single mother in the hood, there was no way they were going to drop it that easy, but I kept doing everything they told me to do.

One afternoon, I was at my sister house and the detectives pulled up with that same old can we talk to you for a minute, now I was not trusting these cops for nothing because every time I trusted them I ended up in jail or losing my kids. Let's face it, nothing good came out of me cooperating so I really didn't want to even hear what they had to say, but because my mom was there and she pretty much made me talk to them. I listened to them though, they wanted me to take a lie detector test to prove once and for all that I had nothing to do with my baby's injury. They would take me down town, and then bring me back after the test, but once again I didn't trust them at all. My mom talked me into it, so I went. I didn't make small talk or look at them; nothing, I just wanted to get it over with and back home as soon as possible!

We arrived at the police station and I got settled in. Another officer hooked me up to the lie detector machine and prepared me to take the test. He started explaining the machine to see how it works and what questions he was going to ask me; a bunch of jazz. I just wanted to tell him to shut up already and give me the test, because this here charade has gone on long enough.

Finally, he begins the test. I think it was about ten questions, and then he unhooked me as another officer took me into a smaller room where we waited for the results which only took minutes. Both detectives came in, I guess they had a question about the test, but said, "we'd like to apologize to you Ms. Jefferson, you passed the test."

I accepted their apology and asked could they take me home, now. They also offered to treat me to lunch on the way home, I declined. At that point, the only thing they could have done for me was gave me my kids back, end of story! But sad to say, I was going to have to fight for them with all my might. I feel, because I was a young black, single female my fight was harder. The social worker on my case fought so hard to keep my kids from me, she did the most like I was the worst mother in the world. The funny thing about her was that, she was the same social worker who allow a white middle age woman, to have seven crack addicted babies before she finally removed them all

Only because she had crack addicted baby number eight, but she fought hard to take mine away for good after I'd proved more than once that I did not hurt my baby, or cause my baby to be hurt. It was an accident plain and simple. That woman gave me hell in, and out of the court room, she tried everything she could to make me out to be a bad mother. If it was up to her I would have never seen my children again, but God. I believe in my heart that the grace of God was all over the situation, and I was never going to give up, even when it seemed like all hope I was lost. I kept my head up and my mind on getting my kids back.

Due to a car accident, that almost cost me my life and right arm, I had money to get what I needed for my kids. I got a house and furniture, and clothes and toys for my kids. The social worker came and checked out my house and was getting ready to set up some visits when I got a call from her saying, "are you ready for your children to come home?"

I dropped the phone. I was so excited, but I hurried and picked the phone back up and said, "yes! What do I have to do?

"Nothing. I will bring them home tomorrow," she said.

I was on the floor crying and thanking God at the news, all I've been praying for was for my children to come home. I stayed up all night and couldn't sleep, I think I got about three or four hours of sleep, but I was still up bright and early in the morning when I got the call that she was on her way with my two oldest children. It seemed like it took her hours even though their foster mother lived only about fifteen-minutes away. I must have looked out my window about a half of dozens of times. The poor window was so foggy looking as if it was the middle of winter.

Finally, I heard the knock on my front door and my son's little squeaky voice; I can't even put into words how I felt. Not only to be able to see, hug, and kiss my babies, but to be able to take them to their room in the house with their mother, where they don't ever have to leave again. I was in heaven on earth while floating in midair. I've waited months to say, "let me show you to your rooms with your toys, and bed, and TV..."

It was surreal, like I was in an awesome dream and scared to wake up and realize this was all fake. I believe I held them extra tight that day. In spite of the battle to get my twins back I was at peace, I had a better outlook of life, and knew that I would continue to do whatever I had to do for my twins to be able to come home. I won this one, and was ready to win the next round, but I had no idea how lucky I was and how much me getting my oldest child back pissed off those social workers. They were serious about keeping my children away from me, and had it in their heads that because of my race and age, I was not fit to raise my twins. The battle was on. I had no time to even enjoy having my oldest home because CPS started their attacks right away and they refuse to stop.

They pulled out all the stops, these people even had my twins' father, who was incarcerated speaking out against me in court, they were asking my family if they thought I could have gotten mad enough to shake my child; if I got angry to quick? And the hurtful thing about, the person who said something, was a person who I looked up to. She answered, that she doesn't think I would hurt my baby on purpose, but out of anger I would shake my child. I'm the one who would get into it with family because I wouldn't let anyone physically discipline any of my children.

Really? It was like a stab in the front, forget the back. I felt like that person stabbed me in my heart because out of everybody, she knew what my kids meant to me and how much I loved them because they're all I had in my life. It was a reason behind me having them and I wanted all my kids. They were mine to love forever. I never knew that anyone who knew me could single handedly work with the enemy to keep my babies away from me. It was horrible how the little bit of my family got involved in my fight to get my babies and it wasn't to help me when it came time to do something that would help me get them back.

All I seen was their backs. Yes, I was angry, my blood was boiling and I promised I was going to take notes and put down names who help create this living nightmare I was in. I was never going to forgive them not ever, they were dead to me. Who, what family? But crazy as it may seem, my heart wouldn't let me keep hating them, yes, I was hurt and mad as hell but I just couldn't with a clean conscience, hate them. I remember when this all started, and they took my babies; I was so hurt and talking to my mom and she told me, "baby girl, everything happens for a reason."

I didn't understand how taking my children from me would have a reason other than to cause me pain, but it was later on in life that God gave me understanding. I will share that revelation later on I promise you it's worth the wait. Months have passed, and I was keeping my supervised visitations with the twins who lived with two different families, my baby girl stayed with a foster mom who had took in many children, she was African American. I loved her so much from the first time we've met, I meant she was so inviting to me; we talked almost the whole time I was there and she let me love on my baby girl never looking down on me. She was like another mom to me. I thank God for her even now, my baby girl has sickle cell anemia and this disease requires much attention. My baby had to endure a lot of pain, test running, and hospital stays, and her foster mom was there through it all.

She was like her angel here on earth, and she always kept me undated on how my baby, our baby was doing. I was very happy with her being in my child's life, but my baby boy on the other hand, did not have such good luck with the families they were putting him with. All of them were far out and Caucasian, not saying they can't take care of a black baby, they just weren't doing such a good job. They were not feeding my baby, not combing his hair, they didn't even put lotion on him his ashy black skin. He actually got hurt bad in one of the homes they put him in and the social worker had the nerves to try to keep me from going to the hospital.

I think I told her off so bad she sat down and was quiet for the rest of my visit, and just when I thought it could not possibly get any worst, the doctor who I am still thankful for to this day came in the room and informed me that my son was in danger. He told me that my son did not have a seizure, and that he passed out due to the blunt force injury to his head. At that time, I know now God had to be holding me because I wanted to rip that social worker's head off her body and throw it in the street with moving traffic, but something came over me. A peace in the mist of the storm and I cried hard praying to God to just let me have my baby back.

I knew that God was a miracle worker and I've seen that with my own eyes. When my baby boy was in ICU with swelling on his brain, my father's girl friend told me to make a cross on his forehead and ask God to lift the blood; and on the next day, not next week but the next day, his brain stopped swelling and he was able to leave the ICU. He was able to be moved to another room, so I knew my God was and still is a miracle worker, and I prayed like never before.

    After that, I just knew I was going to walk in that court room and get my babies back due to recent events. They would just turn my babies over to me, but no I was so devastated and wanted to die; I just didn't understand how they could keep my babies from me like I was a threat to them. I was so confused? I had been proven innocent, not guilty. I never hurt my baby, but the court system still feels like they could do better. It made me sick to my stomach and I was about to give up, but I couldn't. I was literally losing my mind, and one day a visit with my baby girl changed my whole life. It was like any other visit I held, played with my baby and talked to her foster mom about what was going on. When she told me that she knew what happen to my baby boy and that she thinks they are never going to give me my babies back, I believed her.

    She had been a foster mom for a while and had seen it all, plus me and her and my babies had such an awesome bond I just trusted her with my whole heart. So, she went on to tell me that, if I would give up my parental rights she promises me that she will go to court and get our babies out the system and that she would never cut me out of their life, they would always know I'm their mom. I was kind of scared about giving up my rights because there was no guarantee that the courts would award custody to her. It just seems like they were so against me that I had no other choice, my son was not being threated right and was getting hurt.

    I did ask God to give them back to me. My brain was over loaded and I was scared to make the wrong decision, so of course I told some of my family members who thought that it was a bad ideal and that she was just trying to take my babies. But my heart was telling me different. I respected her so much, and I honestly just wanted my son to be with his sister, safe and loved; so, if she did take them at least they would be together. I didn't care about me anymore and my babies deserved to be together, in a home with someone who loved them more than me. I bypassed what the family said and I listened to the love I had for my babies.

    The next court date had arrived and I was ready. Surprisingly, I wasn't nervous at all. I went with a smile on my face, and when it came time for me to speak I loudly, and boldly said, "I give up my parental rights. I signed my rights away."

Right then, a peace just came over me like, wow. The look on their faces especially, the social worker; she had that we won look, but little did they know that victory was my babies. I walked out light and went home. Not even a week passed when I got a call from my baby girl's foster mom Mrs. White, saying I got our babies…. I couldn't form any words to say, I was yelling and crying because it was one of the best days of my life. I could hold them whenever I wanted to and see them whenever I wanted to, no more of anyone hurting my baby boy… I tell you God answered my prayers in a mighty way. It was done.

I was free from the system that kicked me and held me down for years. No more social workers moving me, taking my kids, allowing someone hurt my babies, or to answer too. For the first time in my life, since I was in my early teens I didn't have to worry about CPS, social workers, or the court telling me what to do, how to do, or what they thought was best for me or my babies. It was a freedom like no other, imagine how a person would feel that first day free after being locked up for ten years or more? If I could speak to each one of them that was on my case, the judge, social workers, even some members of my family, I would tell them about themselves.

I would explain to them how it felt to be treated like I was a criminal, how it felt to watch your baby get hurt and treated bad, and not be able to do a thing because you were deemed unfit; even though you were cleared of any wrong doing and found to be innocent. But because of reasons that are unknown, you still had to fight, and fight to be a mom to your children. Oh, my goodness, I would give them all an earful because to them, I was just another case number and not a human being who lost her reasons for living, yeah, I would tell them. I have forgiven them though and moved on with my life and with all my children in my life. But due to me having to give up my rights, my twins had a good life, my baby girl had and still do have the best medical care, more than I could have ever given her.

There you have it, EVERYTHING HAPPENS FOR A REASON…. She was not supposed to make it past twelve years old says the doctor, but through God she is now twenty-two years old and living good. My twin boy is now in the marines living his dream when the doctor said he will be mentally challenged. There is nothing my God cannot do!!! Just trust and believe…

Luke 1:37 King James Version (KJV)
³⁷ For with God nothing shall be impossible.

Jeremiah 32:27 King James Version (KJV)
²⁷ Behold, I am the LORD, the God of all flesh: is there anything too hard for me?

    Having all four of my children back in my life was the best thing God could have ever done for me. It was like, I could breathe again and my life had meaning again. I was ready to prove to my children that I could be a good mother to them and also, to prove to God that he made the right choice when he answered my call, but as ready as I was it was still hard. I had a six-year-old who I swear been here before, she was a little lady if I do say so myself. She walks around giving my four-year-old son, mind you was truly a little old man the business because she played my role better than me at times, but I wouldn't change anything about having my babies back beside them and never had been taken away. The way the police took my children caused more damage than my baby boy being hurt.

    If you ask anyone of them about this case they would probably justify their every move, meanwhile my children wear the mental and psychological trauma on their hearts from a system that instead of doing their job to protect them, hurt them. I still pray hard that God continue to heal me and all my children so history does not repeat itself. I gladly closed that chapter once I decided to stop running from the pain, hurt, and feeling of betrayal when I accepted the challenge to write this book. By doing so, I am force to face the pain it caused me and admit how the situation, the people, and my family members made me feel.

    Then I begin to forgive, even those who I never seen after this whole ordeal was over. I learned how to put the pain to good use and show others that it is possible to trust in God even when it seems like he's not working on your behalf.

The woman inside

One party, two party, three, it never stops; no, it never stops for me.

Fun was meant to have, I was young and a bit sexy, crazy, cool; the beautiful brown eyes with them thick thighs that called all the guys when I dance like a good bump, I had them all on a natural high.

Floating like bees around my honey filled hive waiting for their turn to taste; man, they all wanted just one chance to try.

Then I wake up and realize that to many only want the hive and not the woman inside.

FLASH BACK… FLASH BACK… FLASH BACK…

It was the night of one of the biggest parties I would ever have, my 22nd birthday. I was feeling like I was on top of the world. I had my own house ready for all my babies and a good job, it was looking like tonight was going to be that night. My sister and I had some banging outfits and I had the young weave done right, because I was cold at that and I was the weave dr., my motto was… 'if you can't grow it I'll sew it, if you can't achieve it I'll weave it.' The kids were down stairs with their little sister, the bath tub was full of ice and drinks, the food was nice and the DJ was ready to jam all night.

The party was great, even my mom and her crew showed up. I know some of you are like her mom, yes child, she came in with her all leather suit looking like she was our sister and all the young men were hitting on her, it was so funny. I actually had a guy say, "hey lil momma who party is this?"

"It's my birthday party."

"Okay, happy birthday."

"Thanks."

"Hey, who is that lil sexy over there, can I get that?"

"Fool, that's my mom," I said laughing.

Laughing also, he said, "dang, you gone look like that when you get older…

I laughed so hard I almost use the bathroom on myself. I think we did that because it was a fire party, but sad to say I never had another party like that again. Yet, I was so glad that I had the opportunity to enjoy that birthday….

FLASH BACK… FLASH BACK … FLASH BACK…

In 2000, I gave birth to another beautiful girl who I named after my biological mother, my adopted mother, and her God mother Lena. She was a namesake, I wanted to pay respect to those three ladies who played major roles in my life. It was all a shock to me because I thought I couldn't have any more kids, and it's been five years since my last birth; and I wasn't being as safe as I should've been. I had become kind of what the senior saints would call, loose. The years of unwanted touching and molestations had turned me into a chic I didn't recognize. It was all about what can you do for me.

I felt like I had the upper hand and I wanted to keep it, but even having the upper hand didn't stop me from feeling like trash and unworthy sometimes, so to make myself feel good I played the part and played it well. I once was again, a chameleon as something broke inside of me as the years went on. The constant fighting to stay afloat was wearing me down, and now here I was going to be a mother again; I was confused. What, a baby in five years? And of course, it's me. From the beginning, nothing has come easy for me, not even this pregnancy. I was put on bedrest at four months in, lost my job and had to move back in with my mother, once again. It was hard.

I was very grateful for still being able to go back home when I needed it. That made life a little easier for me, and help kept me sane because besides the pregnancy, I was also dealing with the other reason I had to move back home. It started before the pregnancy, and making a long story short, I got back in touch with my uncle, one of my mother's brothers. He was the one I stayed with and who was only giving me $150 out my check, and taking the rest for himself. Yeah, that's the one; who allowed me to rent in his single-family house, the one I grew up in. Well, some of my childhood was spent there.

I was cool with my kids having their own rooms, and it also came with furniture which was a happy bonus. I got a new job and was living the good life; had a piece of car that got me and my kids around and everything seemed ok. Until, I started noticing little things, like someone being in my house when I wasn't there and things coming up missing, squirrels getting in the upstairs part of the house because of a broken window. My dear old uncle didn't think it was important enough to fix, so I overlooked that and kept on living in my own home; and my kids liked it. Yeah, I didn't want to move anymore, but as we know all things come to an end and that it did.

So, here I was working like a mad woman because I wanted to do something with my kids. I went to get about a hundred dollars out of my bank account and was rudely told I don't have any money in my account. WHAT, YOU GOTTA BE JOKING? But oh, no. She was telling the truth, someone had taken some of my checks and cleaned out my bank account, I was so done. I went home to look under my mattress and realized that food stamps were also missing, and some blank checks. There's only one person who could have did this and I rather not say who, but of course nothing happened to him. I was the one who had to wait five months for the bank to send me a refund check for my money, and that was it.

No one said a word to him, and as a matter of fact, I was told I should've put important stuff up like that, and yet everyone knew that he'd been sneaking in and out of my house since I've been there. The straw that broke the camel's back though, was when my uncle came over my house unannounced and I was gone on vacation, my sister was there with our kids. He just came in without knocking or anything. Needless to say, my house poses to been a mess, there were diapers down the basement stairs and the kitchen was a mess, says my uncle.

I was gone on my vacation which I feel I deserves, and far as I was concern he should have contacted me before even entering my home, but because he did that pop up visit, it became a big mess. When I got back home my uncle and I had a talk about his visit among everything else, and from that conversation I was pretty much told I had to leave. I was so confused, like what just happen here? See, when it rains it really pours, because now I found out I was expecting again and I only had one place to go; back home with my mom, little sisters and brother. So often, I was let down by my so call biological family, and I ran to the family God give me. In truth, wasn't such a loving place all the time.

At times I felt my sisters didn't want me there, from the conversation I wasn't supposed to hear, but it were loud and clear, and hurtful, but I understood it in my own way. I realized that they were young and wasn't just supposed to adjust to me being there because they were little. Not to mention, there have been some uncomfortable, hurtful, and very heartbreaking events that has taken place that rocked all of our worlds. As much as I was affected, I'm pretty sure they were too. The tension in the air somedays was unbearable, but I had nowhere else to go, and had to stick it out for my kids because they didn't deserve to be homeless or out on the street.

So somedays, I'll just lay in the bed and cry, I never really left my room much because I was depressed and hurt. Still to this day I don't think they have a clue of how much they hurt me. I remember I was good at hiding my feelings from everyone, even those who've hurt me. I felt like I deserved it for breaking up their family, I mean, if I was never there he could have never done what he'd done and their family would still be together; and they're lives wouldn't have been turned upside down.

Anyway, getting back on track. I moved back in with my mom and was pregnant at the time and I was not ready. Recall it being five years since I had my twins, and I only had them for six weeks before they were taken from me. Personally, I was like… "NOOO PLEASE GOD HELP ME, I DON'T KNOW WHAT TO DO WITH NO BABY!!!!!!"

But I guess God was like, you better find out quick because that baby did not want to stay in my belly. My cervix was starting to thin at five and a half months and I was having mild contractions; and at six months I had a mild stroke. It was to the point that I was admitted to the hospital at eight months and had to undergo a series of steroid shots because that little girl was ready to come out, but her lungs were not strong enough. I had to stay overnight for about three days, and received shots in my thighs so my little bundle of joy would be ready to come on out. Thank God that the treatment worked, she was healthy and ready to come out and at eight and a half months she was born. I was excited.

When I got home with her it was an uphill battle. I was still on bedrest but I couldn't stay down and was so ready to go back to work; I was living in my mother's home and I had three children with me. I knew I had to get back in my own home. So, soon as I was able I got a job I wasn't playing, Summerfest here I come. Summerfest is a big festival here in Milwaukee that happens at our Lakefront every year. It is games, food, music, and plenty of fun. I was given a security job and I worked all the festivals and it was about five.

I worked all shifts many times because I was trying to get back on my feet. To make a long and boring story short, I worked every job I could get hired and finally, after moving to a friend's houses I was able to get my own house. It wasn't all that, but it was home; and I tell you what, my kids were happy to be in their own home and that's all that mattered to me. My rolling years were for sure rolling fast, I was twenty-six years old with five children, three of them lived with me. I had no man in my life but plenty of male friends and a piece of job just barely making it. I know for sure that I was going down the wrong path, but I had no one to help me get on track. I can't say back on track because from the time I became a mother I was already jacked up.

I was a mother because I was looking for love in all the wrong places, mainly on my back with my legs open because at a young age, that's the only way I knew how to be loved. I never had my dad tell me he loved me, or watch out for those boys, nothing; I just didn't know how a man was supposed to treat a woman he claims that he loves. All I knew was men have been doing whatever to get in between my legs since I was about thirteen years old, so I start to give in. Some gave me gifts, paid my rent, brought me and my kids clothes, food, and even a car, but at the end of the day I still felt used and abused.

My body and mind grew tired, and I just wanted to give up, but my children kept me going. They were my motivation to get better and to do better, and for a while it worked; I was doing better and my life was going well, end of story. Yeah, right. I wish, and I don't want to lie because I was a hustling, slick talking, do anything for a dollar kind of chic. I was not proud of it at all. I did things I said I would never do again, and then went and fell on my face crying to God.

Over the years, I've found out that change must come from within and with no lip service. My definition of <u>LIP SERVICE</u>: to say something but not actually do it. To pretend that you believe a certain thing but not practice that belief. I'd been doing for years, handing out lip service like it was dollar bills and slanging it like I was a baller, and then cry about it on the low behind closed doors. I told myself I was going to do the rolling years right and be that woman. My definition of <u>THAT WOMAN</u>: an independent woman with a good head on her shoulders that's about her business. Taking no shorts from anyone. Yet, I ended up being that chic, a lady who's used her pain to get over on others, and used what she got to get what she wanted without a care in the world.

Oh, how I hated being her, she was created over the years without me knowing, sort of speak. I know it sounds a little off, like how didn't I know? But I'll tell you the truth, I didn't know and I had to have a what the seasons saints call, COME TO JESUS MOMENT. I needed something to happen in my life that forced me to look at who

I've became and made me cry out to JESUS for help. I knew that was the only way I was going to be able to keep living. I know I've been through hell and back a few hundred times as a child and a teenager, but that was beyond my control and I know that no matter how bad it got I know God was covering me. Holding me and sometimes carrying me, but now this is hell that I created.

    Me; no one else but me, and I had to own up to it and repent. To ask God for forgiveness and turn from my wick ways or my life was going to get worst, and that's if I even made it another year. It came to me one day I was growing up! I was starting to think like a woman and now I was weighing my options, dotting my I's and crossing my t's. Oh, my goodness! I was twenty-seven and starting to see me. I know you're probably thinking, wow, twenty-seven, you were supposed to have been grew up, but keep in mind, when a person goes through what I've went through at such a young age, one or two things could happen:

1. Because of the hell life dealt them, that person could take it and allow it to mold them into a motivated, hardworking, determined, winner who will never give up.

OR

2. That person could become me, a chameleon because instead of growing, I regressed. I was too busy trying to just stay afloat and I wasn't real with myself or anyone else; I hid my true feeling and stayed away from the real so I could try and dodge the hurt. This caused me to be childlike in many areas in my life. I became a little girl in a woman's body, but now, I'm becoming a woman without warning, starting to understand what I really want out of life, and how I can get it. I know that there were four turning points in my life that after each one I could never go back, and as a matter of fact, I was pushed to go forward. Sometimes going forward was more painful than going backward but life goes on. The fourth point will come later on, but it was just as important as the first three, later on, you'll see.

Point #1 The year I lost my mom. I was nine and that TURNING POINT was totally out of my control and made me realize at a young age that no one is promised forever! I was pushed into life without the one who gave birth to me before she could teach me how to be a woman.

Point #2 The year I turned into a teenage girl. I was put into many dark situations because some sick men thought that it was a good ideal to violate a young girl while killing her spirit, her self-worth, and trust. At that moment, the little girl was silence, used, abused, and broken. I was robbed of the chance to ever be a normal child again and this left the little girl in me crying out to be a kid, but the actions take that away.

Point #3 The beginning of my rolling years. I was in between a young adult and still not over being a teenager. I was a single mom and had to start learning how to be a role model for my girls; and since my son's dad wasn't around for him, I had to try to teach him how to be a man. Everyone knows a woman can't show a boy how to be a man, but most of all, I met someone and had a life altering relationship with for ten years. The things that relationship put me through pushed me hard, and forward.

No Moore

Your love had me ready to fall from the first time I gave you my digits and what, you really called.
Your looks were true perfection, your body soft but hard, and felt like I was touching liquid gold.
Your skin so dark and smooth and rich, made me want to just bite into your Hershey kisses and never leave from your sweet-smelling bliss.
Man, I had it bad, I was done whenever you called, I did whatever to show you my all. I was hooked you know, locked to you as if I was the chain; you were the lock and key, but my love wasn't enough to keep you beside me. All you had was lust, so when she came along my chain became too small for your key and you choose to let me down slow so you could have your cake and eat it to. All on the low without thinking about the pain you caused, you just kept going until I decided to leave ten years later, it helped me to even the score…
But still I was left with nothing because I got bitten by a brother with the last name Moore….

The Moore Season

It was a hot summer day and me and my crew was dressed cute, out cruising looking for something to get into when a car full of guys pulled up next to us. They yelled out the window trying to get us to pull over, but of course we played hard to get and made them chase a little bit before we pulled over. The driver pointed me out and asked me to come here, now I must say I was shocked, I was in the car with my two beautiful girls. My sister was light skinned with long hair, cute as ever; and my cousin was the same complexation with a huge butt that made all the guys drool. And yet, this cat wanted to talk to me. Wow, I wasn't really into him, but I was tripping because the one with the car and money wanted to talk to me… hey now!

So, we exchanged numbers and all of us had planned to meet up at my cousin's house. The time seem like it went fast and we were running around my sister's house getting ready; yeah, we were already cute but we had to fleshing up and change it up. Hey, we were hot chic's that's how we rolled so…… Mr. driver picked me up and we left, we were going to meet the rest of the click there, so we talked a little while riding. He stopped at the liquor store, and then we stopped outside this white house where a tall dark-skinned guy came out; I could barely see him but it was just something about him.

He opened my door so he could get in and while he was getting in our eye's locked for a brief second, and in my head out of nowhere I heard, *"that's your husband."* For the first time, and I don't know why but I just fell in love with that man right there. I didn't know who he was or what he was, I just knew something in me wanted him. I know I sound crazy, but for real I heard that in my head loud and clear, and since this is no fairy tale we did not get together that night, or the next night, or the next. We barely talked that night because everyone was too busy trying to hook him up with our friend, and it was the funniest thing I ever seen. This man wasn't going, and said he had a tooth ache because he wasn't trying to talk.

I never in my life seen a guy pass up sex, it just wasn't heard of in my world, but it was so obvious he wasn't feeling her and I had other things to worry about. I had to act like I was feeling his cousin who was trying hard, we talked for a while and he seemed very cool, but I just wasn't feeling him at all. After that night, the guys hung out with us a few more times than they were gone. I was kind of bombed because I didn't get a chance to find out what that man had over me.

    Time had passed, I want to say maybe about a year or so, and my sister called me and she said, "sister, guess who here?" For some strange reason I thought about him. I was really praying she said it was him, and in a way my prayers were answered because she said, "…. DRUM LINE PLEASE……… you remember the dudes we meant on 27th street?" I was like yeah, with a big Chester cheese smile and the rest is history. She gave them my address and we all started to kicked it and had some fun again. This time, everyone paired me up with the driver and my good friend with my future husband, and my bestie Lena with his brother.

    We all had a good time, but it started to get kind of awkward because the driver dude had an already girl and a baby, and I just was not feeling him anyway. Lena and Mr. Moore's brother, Mr. blue was really feeling each other, and his brother my future husband was with my friend, and he wasn't feeling her at all. It turned out to be like one of those scandalous movies of who sleeping with who, no one but Lena and Blue were with who they wanted to be with.

    After a while, I stopped talking to the driver and started hanging out with my cousin and her dude which lead me to finally hooking up with Mr. Moore! We talked every chance we got. He called me while he was at work, and he use to sneak over my house by himself and those days were magical. We talked about everything, it was like we always had something to talk about. He would sneak over all the time and we just talked and talked, you would think we would run out of things to talk about say, but nope, we never did. At least not then. In between our talk sessions we shared a little more about each other and that's where my five-year surprise came from.

    But at that time, we were only homie, lover, friends, with friends being the key word. Nothing changed, and as a matter of fact, we lost touch with each other during the time I moved back in with my mother. It wasn't until I had my baby girl that we got back in touch with each other, and not on purpose. Funny story, I was sitting on the porch at my mom's house and all the sudden I see him walking with a book bag across the street. I was shocked at first, I almost let him go but I called his name and he looked up and from that day forward we stayed in contact. He came over to spend time with Lil Bubbles, that's what he called her and we just stayed cool.

He eventually took her to see his mother and step-father. She fell in love with her grand baby and was a pillar in my baby's life, and this came in handy because Mr. Moore decided to move out of town with his brother to better himself, so I was told. I was surprisingly okay with that because my baby's grandparents were awesome, and they helped me so much with her; we were blessed. I never understood why he left, but we were never a couple, so I just got over it and time went on. It was April of 2002, two weeks before my baby turned two years old when out of the blue he shows up knocking on my mother's door like he never left and that was all she wrote; we became a couple.

Now, it was not that easy and we went through a lot of what if conversations, but at the end of the day it was a, let's help each other out situation that pushed us into a relationship. I was truly in love with him, but he was definitely not in love with me at first, I think I grew on him. While I was growing on him, he was doing some growing of his own. I spent seven years being his girlfriend and three years being his wife, and I spent most of all those years sharing him with other women, his family, and his drinking habit. I was always competing with someone or something, even when I didn't know it. That relationship was turning point #3.

I never in all my years was ever treated like he treated me. I would go around his family and they all calling me his wife, and smiled in my face while laughing behind my back because he had just had his other girlfriend over there. He would do things like, go out of town with the family and I couldn't go because it wasn't any room. I will never forget the last time he went out of town and I just so happen to come across pictures of him and some girl all over his mother phone; but then they would come back and chill in my house knowing this. I guess family do stick together whether that person is right or wrong.

The fact that he was spreading his, thinner than a mint cookie self around still didn't push me to leave him. I stayed year after year putting up with him never wanting to be around me and him not coming home. It was a constant battle in my house because he swore up and down that while he was out messing around on me I was cheating on him. He had everyone thinking I was just doing him so wrong and all the while I was at home with the kids waiting on him; sometimes with no food in the house. He would go to one of his many females' house to eat. He would do things like, say he was going to the store and I wouldn't see him for two three days.

No call or anything, and then he had the nerve to come home and have an attitude with me. This would create a hostile situation so he would have a reason to leave again and like a dummy, I would cry when he did leave. I would follow him, try to fight the other woman, and I would even fight him just to get him to stay. I would spend all my money on him and walk around with low self-esteem because he stayed calling me fat and bald headed. His nick name for me was, 'funny looking dude,' and it was so funny to him. For seven years I walked around like it was okay, but I was so dead inside. I found myself addicted to marijuana and food because it was my escape from the reality of my life. Being with that man was killing me because he showed me no love and I don't think he even loved me at all?

I was just convenient for him, he didn't have to work or help me in the house; he had it good and he took advantage of every bit of it. I was sinking in late 2005, and on the verge of killing myself. I just couldn't do it no more, I was having nightmares of being raped all over again. It was so bad that I could not have sex with him, and instead of him understanding he got mad. He would fight me saying I was cheating and he would take my car and be gone until the next day when I had to go to work. I was trying so bad to hold on to nothing, and my addictions were getting worst, until one day we met with a pastor and his family at a gas station. The car we had would not start, and the funny thing was we never had a problem with that car until that day.

No one would help us, he offered to pay people, but no one would help until this guy pulled up and asked did we need some help. He got our car started and wouldn't accept no money and instead, he said, "hey, I got a little old hood church right over there, why won't you go home get the kids and come visit us? Come just as you are."

To my surprise, we went home and got the kids, and then went to church. It was great! I mean, I felt at home soon as I sat down and everyone was so inviting. He was actually smiling and enjoying himself. Wow, I honestly never been to a church like that before. I thank God for that pastor and church; and it still is right now in 2018. My Pastor Rodney E. Campbell, and my church home, Crossing Jordan Ministries. I'm not going to say that my life changed that day all of a sudden, no it didn't. I was still addicted to marijuana and food, and our relationship was at its breaking point, but we both were willing to give God a try.

Then, out of nowhere my addiction to marijuana was done, along with the food. I begin to want to learn more about God and I begin to see the change in me, but as for him, he was still cheating, smoking, and drinking. I use to pray, God please fix him or remove him from my life, and every time I prayed it never fails, I'd catch him in some mess; and like a fool I'd still be with him. I did not understand why, not at that time. I just kept being good to him thinking that if I do this, he would want me or if I get him this, he would want me. It was sick. The fact of the matter is that, he just did not want me, but he wanted a place to lay his head and for a woman to take care of him. Then I realized he did not want me.

It got so troubling that I thought if I cheat on him I would feel better but that just made me feel used and nasty. I did not get any satisfaction out of that at all. It had finally come to the point where we had even moved to a different state trying to make it work and it just did not. I realized that he was damaged. His heart was very damaged and he was dealing with it all wrong by sleeping with different woman, drinking all day all night, and pretty much doing everything to hurt the one who actually loved him. Yet I stayed.

So, we got married. I cannot believe he got worst, and then I knew our time was up and it was time to go. I filed for divorce and never looked back. I had to put that unhealthy relationship to rest before someone, mainly me, killed someone or myself. Needless to say, he is still mad at me for divorcing him. Can you believe he hates me for getting out of something that was killing the both of us? He was drinking himself to death, yet I loved him, but I could not keep watching him do that, and I most definitely could not keep allowing him to break me down any longer.

Yes, we were toxic together, and the older we got the more harmful we become toward each other. I encourage all women and men to not stay in a relationship that is toxic, get out now and do not wait until it's too late. You deserve better than that. I thank God that the damages didn't ruin me for good. I can still love; my heart is not hardening and I don't physically look like what I have been through. THANK YOU, GOD!

It was a long journey, but I learned from it and can take what I have learned and use it to help someone going through what I've went through. I can honestly say that there is a light at the end of the tunnel, and his name is JESUS. There is nothing impossible for Him. While I was in and out of that relationship, I use to look up bible verses and read them out loud. The Bible verses gave me strength, hope, and peace to do what I know I had to do.

Proverbs 3:5-6 (KJV)
[5] Trust in the LORD with all thine heart; and lean not unto thine own understanding.
[6] In all thy ways acknowledge him, and he shall direct thy paths.

    I had to learn to stop trying to understand madness and let go and let God for real. This verse was so hard because, even when I felt like I was following God I was still doing what Charlotte thought was right, and not what God was showing me to be right. So many times, I had found it hard to do right or let go of people and the things God was telling me to let go.

2 Corinthians 12:9-11 (KJV)
[9] And he said unto me, my grace is sufficient for thee: for my strength is made perfect in weakness. Most gladly therefore will I rather glory in my infirmities, that the power of Christ may rest upon me.
[10] Therefore I take pleasure in infirmities, in reproaches, in necessities, in persecutions, in distresses for Christ's sake: for when I am weak, then am I strong.
[11] I am become a fool in glorying; ye have compelled me: for I ought to have been commended of you: for in nothing am I behind the very chiefest apostles, though I be nothing.

His strength is made perfect in weakness this gives me joy because I now know I made it through my most trying times. He was made stronger in my weakness so when the devil tried so very hard to hurt me God said its okay baby girl, my grace is sufficient for thee. Oh, yes, that is so powerful.... Just reading this makes me feel at peace.

    So, my marriage with Mr. Moore was over, but it still had an effect on my child. See, when I said enough was enough I was not thinking about how much it would hurt my child. She was for the divorce and was really upset with him for the way he had been acting before the divorce, mainly the drinking, it was uncontrollable and harmful to not only him, but everyone around that cared about him especially his child. She was not upset with the divorce but more so upset with the fact that once he seen that I was completely done he moved on from both of us. He walked out of her life and started a new one becoming a part time daddy, and his anger with me would spill over to their conversations every time they talked.

It became a very delicate situation to deal with. I prayed often that my baby will heal from the hurt her dad and I cause with our toxic relationship. I kept God as my focus and pushed for my family every day, and that is how I kept my peace; since I left the relationship peace has been easier to find. I still have issues, who don't, but I know from whom my help comes from, so after the fifteen minutes of tearing up and twenty minutes of fussing my peace kick in like, boom! It's like taking a piece of love, mix it in with a dose of joy, and stirring it with a whole bunch of I got this my child so relax. After it was all said and done I left with a feeling of pure uncut peace that comes straight from the MOST HIGH… THE GREAT I AM. He said it in his Word:

Philippians 4:7 (ESV)
⁷ And the peace of God, which surpasses all understanding, will guard your hearts and your minds in Christ Jesus.

Psalm 46:1 (KJV)
¹ God is our refuge and strength, a very present help in trouble.

I am grateful for one thing that came out of that relationship beside my baby girl, that it put me in a position where I had to cry out to God. I could not call my bestie, I could not call my mom, and I could not call my pastor. I had to go to directly to God myself, it was a must. No more faking and no more half stepping, I had to go call on God for myself or that relationship was going to kill me spiritually and physically. I am so grateful for that, and once again I know some may not understand why I was grateful about that, well, the answer is very simple, no bells and whistles. The answer, I was dying inside and everything I was doing was killing me slowly, and not just me but my children as well.

Once I became sick and tired of being sick and tired, I got down on my knees and cried out for God to help me. I cried out many of times, but I always went back and this time my cry was not in vain. I needed

God like never before, and just like Jacob I wasn't letting go until He blessed me.

Genesis 32:24-32 (KJV)
24 And Jacob was left alone; and there wrestled a man with him until the breaking of the day.
25 And when he saw that he prevailed not against him, he touched the hollow of his thigh; and the hollow of Jacob's thigh was out of joint, as he wrestled with him.
26 And he said, let me go, for the day breaketh. And he said, I will not let thee go, except thou bless me.

    I never in my life cried out that hard with all my heart, but it worked. I praised God like never before during the struggle and I continued to praise Him afterward, now that doesn't mean that I am perfect, not at all. I just learned from my mistakes and from my hardheadedness, and in doing so I am able to once again help someone else who need to know that hey, that relationship does not define you. Through God you have the power to walk out and see what a healthy love looks like, as God heals you he will show you real unconditional love. I must say, I ended that chapter of my life on a good note. I was developing a closer relationship with God, and I was strong enough to finally end that hurtful relationship for good and I started to love my self. I was on a good path looking up and I was at peace.

Love letter to God

The feeling of warmth on a sunny day, the perfect way the wind blows a mist of your love my way, the time we shared, the way we loved oh, how much you care.
You make me smile when I want to cry, you make me love without asking, why you are my forever here and now, without you I think I would surely die.

FLASH BACK … FLASH BACK… FLASH BACK…

I often loved having time with my kids and church family, it was like the highlight of my life. One of my favorite memories was my first family night at Crossing Jordan Ministries, I believe the year was 2006, that day was awesome and it was something there for everyone to do. They had the video game on the projector screen, a table out for cards and board games, we laughed and played, and talked all night. The best part was that our pastors Rodney and Serita Campbell, were there right in the mist having fun with us all. We ate and played and just had good family fun until the wee hours of the morning.

It was unreal. I had never been to a church where we could just have fun. The family night didn't stop when we left, and most of the teenagers came to my house and kept me up until about nine in the morning. We played just about every game we had, and then sat up talking. I found out that the teenagers were comfortable around me and that was a plus, it meant that I could keep an eye on mine since everyone loved to come to my house, but that day was amazing. We had many more good times like that, but that one will always stay in my heart because we were new to a fairly small church and everyone knew everyone. They still opened up their hearts to us like they knew us for years and it was a blessing.

If they only knew what I was going through at that time, what they were keeping my mind off of with their huge display of love. That day changed my mind and heart about church for good. It made me realize that with some people what you see is what you get. When I walked into that church, which is my church home now, I got love and my kids got love. We saw real joy, real peace, real happiness, and real acceptance. I really want to thank all that was there at Crossing Jordan Ministries when I joined, you all opened your hearts for me and my kids at a time when we needed it most, and that family night was just a welcome home party to us because I felt like I was at home the first time I walked through the door. God's love was and is still in Crossing Jordan Ministries….

FLASH BACK… FLASH BACK… FLASH BACK…

Church Life… verse… Saved life

As the years rolled by and I got a little up in age, I started to realize that having a church life, going to church whenever the doors opened, always willing to help in many areas as you can, attending every service, but not opening the bible at home, not knowing how to pray for yourself and basically relying on the pastor to get you to heaven was not helping me at all. I was at Crossing Jordan Ministries whenever the doors opened, and never missed a service, whether it was inside or outside, or visiting another church I was there. Churching became almost like a drug to me and I had to have it; I needed it and I was not right if I missed any of it. The rush of the praise and worship kept me in tears, it was as if every song related to my life in some kind of way and I had tears of joy, tears of sadness, tears of thanks every service.

It was like they were only singing to me, then you had the word, sometimes I heard the pastor, but then there were those times when I heard, understood, and knew that word was for me!!!! Man, it was one of those, get your butt in order under the word type of sermons, and it kicked me into reading the word for that moment.

Then you had the offering and tithe part of the service. I was a cheerful giver when I was able to give and sad and embarrassed when I wasn't able to. Then there was the usher board, I loved being on the usher board. My position was to make sure I hugged everyone coming and going from service, and also make sure praise and worship, and all the pastors had towels and water. I also, had to assist those who needed it. I had to keep my eyes open and pay attention to everything that was going on, which in more ways than one hindered my salvation. I was too busy chasing kids, seating guest, getting water, ushering to the bathroom, and making sure those who became overcome with the spirit and emotions were okay.

To hear the word or to worship, or even to pray for myself, I would sometimes be up working the alter during prayer time and end up overcome by the spirit. In other words, I would be on the floor crying out for my soul releasing the I was in pain at that moment. I kept this up for about six years; I would read my bible and join Chop It Up. This was a service where we would all come together, usually on a Tuesday and all who would attend have two minutes to speak on whatever verse from the bible that was picked that evening. It was a chance to say what understanding you gathered from that bible verse.

There also was bible study and Sunday service, and what I understood I tried to live it to the best of my ability, in between my falls. It got to the point where my soul began to want more, and everything my Pastor was preaching started to make so much sense. I wanted to be saved and not just live the churching life, but I wanted to make sure my name was written in the lamb's book of life.

Revelations 3:5 (KJV)
5 He that overcomethh, the same shall be clothed in white raiment; and I will not blot out his name out of the book of life, but I will confess his name before my Father, and before his angels.

Malachi 3:16 (KJV)
16 Then they that feared the LORD spake often one to another: and the Lord hearkened, and heard [it], and a book of remembrance was written before him for them that feared the Lord, and that thought upon his name.

Basically, it got real to me. My kids were getting older and it was becoming harder and harder to convince them to come to church while my relationship was going downhill. Mr. Moore and I, had come to, in my Boys 2 Men voice, the end of the road and it was time for me to get my life in check with God, for real. I was in constant warfare within myself. I was becoming spiritually bipolar and not knowing what was exactly happening to me. One minute I would pick up the bible and read it for a moment, then have an urge to go smoke a cigarette or to call up my pick of the week. A date, new man, or whoever I felt like being bothered with at the moment, it was unreal; but one thing I have learned about the word, is that every answer you need is in it.

Ephesians 6:12 (KJV)
12 For we wrestle not against flesh and blood, but against principalities, against powers, against the rulers of the darkness of this world, against spiritual wickedness in high places.

And this is why I couldn't fight with my flesh. I often felt like it was impossible for me to do, I needed to know what I was up against and by searching the word, I found it. That wasn't all I found, I also went a little deeper and found out…

Romans 7:18 Context (KJV)
[18] For I know that in me (that is, in my flesh,) dwelleth no good thing: for to will is present with me; but *how* to perform that which is good I find not.

When I found this, it was like I found gold, well, I didn't find it per say, yet I heard it in a sermon. That lead to a deeper look in myself, but it explained to me what I was up against, this flesh! And that old good for nothing Satan. I know I use to be pissed off and disgusted with the choices I've made. No one knew how I hated myself; it was like I would get up from the floor crying out to God asking him to clean me and help me, and then go lay up with a man. Or, I would ask God to forgive me for disrespecting his temple, and then I would go light up a cigarette. I was killing myself slowly and wondering why my kids didn't want to give their life to God. I was not a very good representation of living for God or living a saved life. It became so easy at one point to stay the same, but say I was changed? I was single handedly saying God's word was a lie. Why? Because in his Word it says…

2 Corinthians 5:17 (KJV)
[17] Therefore if any man be in Christ, he is a new creature: old things are passed away; behold, all things are become new.

So, there was no way I was living for Christ, yet I was still the old me, snapping and cussing folks out, smoking, and even fornicating. It was impossible to have been saved and still be the old creature. You must understand that I was living a lie, a big lie, but even then, God covered me with his grace and mercy! Which I thank God for even now, because where would I have been if he would have turned me over a reprobate mind showing me no mercy? As I read his word, that is not far from what could have taken place in my life.

Romans 1:28-32 (KJV)
[28] And even as they did not like to retain God in their knowledge, God gave them over to a reprobate mind, to do those things which are not convenient;

²⁹ Being filled with all unrighteousness, fornication, wickedness, covetousness, maliciousness; full of envy, murder, debate, deceit, malignity; whisperers,
³⁰ Backbiters, haters of God, despiteful, proud, boasters, inventors of evil things, disobedient to parents,
³¹ Without understanding, covenantbreakers, without natural affection, implacable, unmerciful:
³² Who knowing the judgment of God, that they which commit such things are worthy of death, not only do the same, but have pleasure in them that do them.

For I knew I was living off that list far too long, but God never left me and I don't want to think about where I would be if he would have left me. Since we're on the subject, I'll just say there are so many places that I could have been, or things I could have done, but God blocked it. I could have been hooked-on drugs, on the street selling my body, in prison, alone never getting my children back in my life, or DEAD.... but guess what? My God BLOCKED IT. He blocked it for a purpose, and I knew I had to figure it out, even if I had to spend the rest of my life doing so. The churching life did not appeal to me anymore and I started to see it for what it was, a stumbling block.

I would be lying if I said that I instantly lined up, or that I never fell again. It was a process for me and I am still on that journey for perfection in God's eyes. Every day is a new lesson waiting to be learned and a new challenge awaits me each day I am blessed to wake up.

My pastor said, "being saved is a process that you must work on every day, for even God knew that we would fall sometimes."

Romans 3:23 (KJV)
²³ For all have sinned, and come short of the glory of God;

This motivated me and also, given me the incentive to seek God more. Not to seek money and a big house, and a nice car, although those things would make my life easier, but I heard if I seek God He would add all that I need, and desire to my life.

Matthew 6:33 (KJV)
³³ But seek ye first the kingdom of God, and his righteousness; and all these things shall be added unto you.

    I had to program this in my head because it was not easy to just trust God, when I was trying to learn how to live in His will. It seemed like when I was doing wrong, I were, but when I started to do right I was lacking the strength. My oldest son said one day, "mom, why do bad things happen to good people?"

    I could not answer that question for nothing in me. I begin to tell him, "it's okay son, God got us no matter what."

    It wasn't until recently I was able to tell my boy, "living God's will brings about some struggle and some pain because this world, and the ugly devil don't want you to live. They want you to die physically and spiritually, but when you are saved and living for Christ, God gives you a peace that passes all understanding in the mist of it all. God never said we wouldn't have problems, issues, heartache, and long suffering, but He did say that He will give us joy that this world can't take. Peace in the mist of the storm, and love that covers all." I was pleased with that answer.

Psalm 18:1-2 (KJV)
¹ I will love thee, O LORD, my strength.
² The LORD is my rock, and my fortress, and my deliverer; my God, my strength, in whom I will trust; my buckler, and the horn of my salvation, and my high tower.

    This is one of my favorite bible verses, because now I know that my God is awesome and this creates a strong belief in me that I can make. Just to know that He is my rock and my fortress makes me feel ten feet tall. To know that I can stand on Him and stand under Him. I don't have to be strong all the time, why? Because He is my strength. The verse just has all the bells and whistles for me and puts me in worship mode because there is no one on earth that can be all things to you always, only God! The more I got into and studied His word the more I thirsted to be saved in His Will, and to be pleasing to Him. Living the churching life was not going to do for me anymore. Deeply, I wanted to go deeper in Him.

It was like my first time every feeling real love. I loved God; I wanted to make Him smile. The realness of how I was feeling was exciting and new. I really knew what the saints meant when they said, "it's like fire shooting up in your bones." I really felt like I had a fire started in my body because I couldn't sit down on it, I had to shout, run, jump, and tell someone how good God was.

Jeremiah 20:8-9 (NIV)
8 Whenever I speak, I cry out proclaiming violence and destruction. So the word of the LORD has brought me insult and reproach all day long.
9 But if I say, "I will not mention his word or speak anymore in his name,"
his word is in my heart like a fire, a fire shut up in my bones. I am weary of holding it in; indeed, I cannot.

The world often will not listen to you when you bring the word of God and the good news of Christ, but as a new creature you cannot hold it in. You cannot keep God and His Word to yourself because it truly is like fire. I found that sometimes just like Jeremiah, some people don't want to hear what I had to say about God and His wonders so they shut me out. They talked about me saying things like she thinks she better than me or us, and if she saved why do she do that, and why you aren't living this way. Who do you think you are? But that fire in me kept me going at times I fell, but I would get back up.

You want to hate on me let me show you some love which often confused fools. I had my moments when I just couldn't because it was too hard, but I also was able to pull up my boot straps and get right back in the race. The big difference came when I started to really trust in God and I still going through it, but I went through it with peace. My tears flowed less and my understanding was on the word. I still work on that hard, so I can stay balanced. Always remembering that we all fall, but to get back up is the key and when you get back up with Jesus you get back up with power. God does not hate you or look down on you because you fell. I believe in His word, it says that a just man falls seven times, and what makes him just is that he gets back up in Christ; now that was food for my soul that helped me continue to grow.

Proverbs 24:16 King James Version (KJV)
[16] For a just man falleth seven times, and riseth up again: but the wicked shall fall into mischief.

    This was well needed to step out of living the churching life and in to living saved. I think that I was riding on my emotions and sometimes I still do, but back then it was all emotions. If I was going through something depending on the song I was crying or either on the floor screaming out to God, or jumping around like my pants were on fire but once I left church none of it mattered. I went back into that situation and continue to allow that situation to control my mind. It was like I only felt the power at church while the singing was going on or when the pastor was preaching hard and the music was playing. My emotions had me on a roller coaster ride that I could not get off of. I was not trusting in God, I was going with my emotions and seeking out that temporary fix like a drug. I did not know any better, I wasn't purposely riding my emotions I just really thought that I was getting close to God and instead of talking to someone I kind of stood on my own understanding. This was one of my biggest mistakes. Once again, if I would have opened the bible for myself I would have seen that God wants us to lean on his understanding not our own.

Proverbs 3:5-6
[5] Trust in the LORD with all thine heart; and lean not unto thine own understanding.
[6] In all thy ways acknowledge him, and he shall direct thy paths.

    I found out the more word you get in you the more your spirit grows, so I started asking questions and I prayed for understanding, the right understanding of His word. I still pray that prayer now because there is so much to learn in His word that no one will ever learn it all. The fire that I had in the beginning of my churching life was real. I still do believe that I met God that day I walked into Crossing Jordan Ministries, and it had nothing to do with the people at that time; it had everything to do with Him setting that meeting up. He made sure that we would meet pastor Rodney and pastor Serita, so I was in the right place at the right time and my courtship with Him would begin.
    God could reach you no matter where you are, but we don't know His plans for our life. It's best to just step aside and let Jesus have

his perfect way in your life. In saying that I come to realize that I got in the way. I begin to ride on my emotions, and I allowed the many situations going on at home to take front stage. I needed an outlet at that time to make living easy for me and that's where it started to change for me, churching instead of living a saved life begin. I used the church as a place to run to but my mind was not in the correct mode to spiritually grow. My worship became, and praise were conditional and my purpose for being at church was more on a job/obligation level.

I had attended, or was going to ushering, get the water, seat the people and make sure everyone was hugged. God took second stage until I realized that I had no connection to God anymore, and it was all on me; I left God. I was slipping farther away from the true reason why I was in church, to live right, learn more about God and hear His word. It was time for me to get my mind, soul, and spirit back focused on Jesus. I was dying inside and I had to get saved for real. My life was taking a turn that did not look to promising; what good would it have been to be in church half your life but die and go to hell.

Church does not keep you from hell, yet your personal relationship keeps you from hell. I needed to talk to God for real. I needed to start living a life that represent who God is in my life. That was one of my come to Jesus moments when I realize that I was going to die, and God would say to me:

Matthew 7:21-23 King James Version (KJV)
[21] Not everyone that saith unto me, Lord, Lord, shall enter into the kingdom of heaven; but he that doeth the will of my Father which is in heaven.
[22] Many will say to me in that day, Lord, Lord, have we not prophesied in thy name? and in thy name have cast out devils? and in thy name done many wonderful works?
[23] And then will I profess unto them, I never knew you: depart from me, ye that work iniquity.

My life took a turn for the better and I started to fear God's meaning, and respect Him and His word. I pushed hard to live the life that God wants us to live. Learning how to love unconditionally and forgiveness was one of my greatest moments in God, so I could not continue to be mad at mom for leaving me, and mad at dad for his mistakes, or even hating the men that took advantage of me. I had to forgive and love no matter what, and pray for them and myself as well. It was not easy. I thought I forgave but then it would come up and I was hating them again. I had to learn that I could forgive someone and still have some hurt from the impact of their action on my life.

I am built with those dang gone emotions that sometimes don't care if I forgave a person or not. The memory is still there and it hurts, but one thing that helped was knowing that it was the past and God got me now. He had me then, and I am sane and still living, able to love... it was for those reasons, and a few more that put the churching life to bed for good. She had a good run, but it's over; no more emotional roller coaster services and no more putting my duties over God. No more side praising. I pushed to live save and I pushed to please God at all cost, not man. I will get better at loving unconditionally and my worship will be coming from a true place for God said:

John 4:24 King James Version (KJV)
[24] God is a Spirit: and they that worship him must worship him in spirit and in truth.

To become a true worshiper with a clean heart and a pure spirit, was and still is what I desire and will always work toward having. I welcomed a saved life with open arms and I never want to let it go. I only want to grow closer to God and be a useable vessel for Him to use as he wishes whether it be to heal, or to help draw souls, or to just be a help to the people in need. I am willing and ready.

My father the super hero

One of the best things that came out of me being saved for real was renewing my relationship with my daddy. Through the years, I always loved my dad and respected him no matter what, but in my heart, I hated his actions during my childhood. I was convinced that he loved my sister more than me always. I never thought that my dad respected me, loved me, was proud of me, or even loved my children. He never said that he didn't love or respect my children and I, he just was never there for me like I seen him be there for my siblings and it hurt. I was the only one of his children that experienced the drug use and unruly unsafe environment that came with living with him.

My older sister had run away and never came back, and my step sister and brother were able to escape it too because their mother took them with her when she moved out. I was left there by myself with no one to turn to and nowhere to go. I carried those feeling of loneliness and sadness and hate for many years, but I always showed my daddy love because I did love my daddy with all my heart; he was a superhero to me, but our relationship never seems to be as close as I wanted it to be. I guess you could say I was very jealous of the relationship he had with his other children, mainly my older sister. Those two were and still are like two peas in a pod. Whereas me and him were like distance cousins in my mind.

As the years rolled on from childhood to adulthood, my dad and I see each other and talked to each many times. I always tried to keep an open line of communication with my dad. That love that I had for my dad was bigger than life because he was my superhero. I had created the perfect dad in my head, but when reality kicked in I sometimes felt like a step child. As an adult, my oldest child asked my father why he always helped my older sister but never helped me? My dad's answer to her was, "I know she got it."

That answer infuriated my daughter and she begin to pull away from my father and always said that she just did not feel close to him. Instead of feeding that ideal I explained to my child that no matter what, my dad is only human, in his eyes it may seem like I always had it because I never showed him that I did not. I was too business trying to seem like I was good to ever really ask him for help. Sometimes I did ask for help and sometimes he would help. I remember some promises he made and never kept, and how when I really needed him he was not there, but then I would just stopped in mid thought and went back to him being only human; flesh and blood. Which meant he wasn't a real superhero and that he was bond to make mistakes and mess up some times.

It took me to get married again to hear the words from my dad that I have been longing to hear all my life. Yes, he told me he loved me and that he was proud of me. I was overjoyed and so emotional that beautiful day. He couldn't have picked a more perfect time to confess that to me. It was like the heavens opened that day and the sun was shining only on us. For the first time in my life I found out the man that I wanted to love me and to be proud of me was actually proud of me and loved me. Our relationship took on a new light and meaning.

I always loved my dad and thought he was bigger than life, but now that I was at ease I didn't have to try hard for his attention because deep in my soul I knew that all I was feeling wasn't true. The past was now the past and no longer controlled my present or future. My dad never knew how I felt and still do not know how I felt about him. I always kept those feeling within to scared that everyone would know that we had no relationship, but if I had a chance to do it all over again I would've sat down with my father and expressed how I felt about our relationship. I would have told him that I did not feel loved or wanted sometimes. I would have told him that he was my superhero and I needed him to be there for me to protect me.

I get so upset with myself at times for not telling him even once I became an adult. I could have told him, but I allow my emotions to keep me from having a real relationship with him, and for that I am sorry. I now believe we have an awesome relationship and I Thank God for it. Nothing can ever take me from my dad, that man got my heart… all of it. He is the strongest man I know physically and emotionally. I watch him go through so many attacks on his health since I was sixteen, and just like a superhero he would bounce back like it was nothing. From cancer to autoimmune disease that almost took him out, and then just recently cancer again where he had to get one third of his right lung taken out.

To see him in the hospital bed after surgery was one of the hardest things I ever had to do, and I have visited him in the hospital even before being in the ICU, but to see him after surgery in all that pain in such a vulnerable state was too hard for me. He is my superhero my comeback king….and on that day I realized, I pray to God every night not soon that one day he won't be here anymore. I will be here without him.

Leaving the hospital that day was bitter sweet for me. I wanted to stay and love on him and for him to hug me, but the sight of how much pain he was in tore me up inside. I had to kiss him and pray with him before I go. I thanked God so much that day for my dad's life, and after that day, maybe three days later the comeback king was out of the hospital and in the streets like, wow. With me nagging on the phone like always, "daddy please get your self-home and rest."

Lol, that man don't know the meaning of rest, lay down, or relax. He was worst then the energizer bunny. I think he would put the bunny out of business. I live for those and give them, *'I just want to hear your voice please get some rest calls.'* Just to hear him on the other end giving me excuses why he can't sit his butt down is priceless to me. We got a special kind of love that I would not change for nothing in this world. I love everything about my dad the way he loves his kids, walks, talk, and dress; a young cat would have a ball in his closet. I understand him now more than I ever did, and I accept him for who he is. My dad, THE SUPERHERO…. kicking all life threating disease's butt with a single blow…able to love all his kids in different ways with one big heart…. never sitting aka, the COMEBACK KING….

The one thing that I am thankful for is that God gave us a chance to have a loving relationship while we are still in the land of the living. We both have faced death many times in our lives…BUT GOD SAW FIT FOR US TO LIVE ON… GIVING US ANOTHER CHANCE TO SAVE OUR RELATIONSHIP. Happy could never express how I feel right now on this day as I write about my dad and I. Elated, excited, over joyed, grateful…....are just some of the words that come to mind, but still not great enough. I guess when God does it there are no words!!!! I like to take a moment to encourage those of you who may be estranged from your mother or father right now, please take it to God.

Now I don't know how great or how small the reason is, but I do know that you only have one set of parents and there is nothing impossible for God. Take it to Him in prayer and remember you too must open your mind, soul, and heart as well. Make that part of your prayer, ask God to first, heal you and soften your heart so you will be in position to accept God's healing in the relationship. Do it for you, you deserve a light heart and a peaceful relationship with your parents. If they are no longer here I give my condolence, but still go to God in prayer and he can still heal you from that situation. With much love to you and your family as I bring this encouragement knowing firsthand that the only way to make it better is to give it to God.

Why

We just started to know each other, and I admit it was a long time coming but still you were taken to soon.
I watched you fall and get back up each time with a little more swearing that your nights were no longer nights but bright fresh noon's.
I stood by your side after every kick life give you cancer, drugs, Lord even your kidneys had a turn to try to take you from me.
But still you rose like the superhero I knew you to be.
But still why Lord was my daddy taken from me;
Why did they hurt him when life already did him in?
Why did they take him when he fought so hard to be here for me?
Tears they fall every time I think of how they so rudely ripped my superhero away from me.
Lord why, why, why did you let them take my daddy from me????

This is truly the hardest thing I ever had to do, to have to write how someone could be so cruel, malicious, so diabolical is the hardest thing to do. I don't want to give those who did this devastating act to my family any glory, but I have to finish the story of my superhero who even in death is still my superhero.

On January 18th my father was found murdered and left like an old rag hanging in a basement of a known drug house. My father was torture and burnt alive the day before his birthday. Someone hated my dad so much that they did not just take his life, but torture him as well. Now let's be real about the situation, my father had money and cars that many people wanted, even the woman he took care of for years. So, it's not really a mystery why he was murdered.

After his death things started disappearing like all his cloths, money, and even some of his cars. People who have always been there started to become unavailable and defensive. It was madness. Everyone worried so much about the money etc. leaving my sisters, aunt, and I, to deal with the unbelievable pain of losing him. This happened in 2018, but it still hurts like someone just stumped on my heart. Some days I cannot sleep and the fact that those responsible for his murder were never caught leaving me with constant panic attacks.

I am so blessed to have had the bond that we gained and that my children had a chance to have a relationship with my dad before this tragedy took place.

Rest in peace dad your girls got this, and we will not rest until the ones responsible for this are caught. Love you so much my SUPERHERO.

Free

I no longer want to be what everyone wants me to be….no I just want to be my talkative, fun loving, much to say, opinionated, sometime needing the last word me.
I no longer want to live for others I just want to live for me…. I want to talk like I want however I want, love who and how I want, dress how I want, and even not talk when I want Lord I just want to be me.
I no longer want to care about someone else feeling when mines don't matter…I just want to be free to walk away without feeling disrespectful, or be able to stop a conversation without it being the end of the world Yes. Lord I just want to be me.
Lord I just want to be free because it's too hard to keep trying to get people to understand me.
So, Lord I just really need to be free…....

Womanhood

The older I got the more I started to accept who I became, you know all of me the good, bad and the ugly, and I begin to truly love me. I mean for the first time in my life I started to see me in a whole new light. I was so use to hiding everything from everyone that at some point I lost who I was, it became hard to see me from all the bull I was slinging trying to be what everyone else wanted me to be. I know it was no one's fault that I played make believe more than half my life, but that was my defense mechanism, my way of keeping my soul and emotions safe, so I thought. Some good that did, I still became a bipolar emotional ball of mess, looking for the easy way out of life.

The fact that I had been hurt by just about everyone that I loved and called family played a major role in my chameleon lifestyle for so long that I delayed my own growth and caused womanhood to arrive late. Yes, I was a mother and yes, I looked like a full-grown woman, but that child that never got to be a care free child was lost, and refuse to grow up. The title of this book means so much to me because I was a child lost, I wanted to be a child, but at times I could not. I had to be so many things for so many people that I dare not enjoy childhood not even the little bit that I had. At times I was able to just be a kid and I loved it, but right around the corner there was life just waiting to steal my joy once again.

Things often happened so close to me in my life that it seems like it was made believe, an unreal bad movie with part one and part two, so the child I was supposed to be hid inside me and the woman I became carried the child I couldn't be. The child that was lost my whole life made it hard for me to even act like an adult sometimes. I was always unsure of who I was. It was like a child in a grow up's body yeah, I looked the part and even talked the talk to play the part well, but inside I was as lost as a blind person taking a route they never took before. I was just stuck feeling around until I found someone to help me, then on to the next step.

It was years of confusion, self-hatred, hiding my truth, and play acting going on until I found me through Jesus. Once I became closer to God womanhood did not scare me as much, and it became easy for me to accept me enough to want to grow and change for the better. My walk with God helped me understand how much what I was doing was hindering me from growing up. It was time to let the woman inside me take the front seat and allow God to drive. I had to step out of the way of my growth and future success.

I was no longer just a CHILD LOST, I had finally become a WOMAN full body, mind, spirit, and soul. I was on my way to being free, totally free with no limits, no boundaries, free, and I was so happy that I started that process. It was a long time coming, twenty-nine years to be exact. The road I was on was full of turns, ducks, and drives, but I had a good feeling that it was going to be worth all the bumps and bruises, and I was right. I am now walking into womanhood completely at forty-three and a half and it feels greats. I truly believe that my success will continue to grow as long as I stay strong in my walk with God, for I credit my growth to my relationship with God. Tell me who else has the power to show you who you are, but God!

I am Woman hear me roar………

Sisterhood

You got my back girl I got yours ride or die females taking over blocks in the city I bet my sister cooler than yours.
Played together worked together and you know we hated together, if we fall we all fall that's how close we hang together.
Like a small gang we were all about the same but in different ways, ups and downs split us but due to love couldn't keep us apart
True ride or die chicks our click was lit, but as we got older our click turned to you on your own chic.

I was blessed to have one sister from my mom and dad, one sister from my dad and step mom, and four sisters from my adopted family. Our sisterhood always came with some love, conflict, jealousy, competition, and support. My relationship with my oldest sister was not as strong as I always wished it could be and after our mother died I needed her, but she was only twelve at that time and she did not take it well. Once she got of age to leave and not come back that's just what she did, I believe she was about fifteen-sixteen years old and I was devastated. We didn't have the best relationship, but she was all I had. My big sister was the one who was supposed to teach me about boys and life, but I guess she had to do what was best for her and dragging your little sister along was not a good ideal.

Then comes my baby sister my dad's little ball of sun shine, she was so cute, but she gave me hell like any little sister would do to their older sister. I stayed in trouble behind that little girl, but she was so cute I couldn't stay mad at her. We had a love hate situation going on, yep I loved her to life, but hated her at the same time because she made my life miserable, lol. I was being punked by a toddler. Around the age of thirteen I was blessed with four more sisters from my adopted mother and I was the oldest by some months. In the beginning it was so fun we did everything together, me and my sister who was right under me because we were best friends before my mom died.

It was like we just rekindled our old friendships. As children, we played together, hung with friends together, danced together, and of course got in trouble together. We sometimes let our little sisters join in the madness with us food fighting with the boys in our hood who stayed on our porch while mom was working. Playing hid go get it, sneaking boys in the house and just about getting caught all the time. Yeah, we were no angels, but we had each other's back. We fussed at each other like sister often do, but when we were young nothing was bad enough to keep us apart.

Once adulthood started to creep around the corner things got real. Our younger sisters, it is three of them, started to step into who they were with a little bit of freedom.

Then, it happened, the first fight between me and two of my adopted sisters. It was so silly and over a monopoly game; my sister and I argued about it and then it turned physical. I had to fight two of them that day while I was very pregnant. I never said anything about it after it happened, but I was so hurt I could not believe that my little sisters who act like they love me and look up to me would put my unborn baby in danger. That incident put a scar on my soul. Still to this day talking about it makes me feel some type of way, but I pushed pass that and put on my, I'm okay face and move on like everyone else did. My younger sisters and I have a good relationship now. I don't want to destroy what we have now because I came along way to get here with all of them and I myself may have offended my sisters in some kind of way at some point of time in our journey together.

I have been through more pain then I show on the surface, and I just want to get it out so that a light can shine in such a dark situation. I have been subjected to fights, talking behind my back, turning their back on me, making me feel like I and my kids were a burden, but in the mist of it all we have grown so much. We love each other so much, and for that alone God I am so grateful. To have a close sisterhood that no matter what our relationship is good, bad, or ugly at the moment we would all drop whatever to go see about each other.

January 23rd, 2018 I was rushed to the emergency room because it wasn't looking to good and my husband called my family to tell them what was going on. They had my brain scanned, and then scanned it again, and as we sat there waiting the doctor gave us the news that I had a stroke. My right carotid artery was clogged, and they needed to get me to St. Luke's ICU right away. My Dad was the first to come and by the look on his face as him and my husband talked, I knew it was serious. The pain was enough to bring an elephant to their knees, my face was swollen, my vision was blurry, and I could not keep my balance.

Once I was moved to St. Luke's I was rushed to get an MRI and CAT scan to take more pictures of my brain and while all of this is going on I notice that one by one all my sisters yes, all six of them show up with their families. I don't think they know how my heart was overjoyed. I felt so blessed that not one, but all would come to check on me. When it counts we have each other's back, because we are human and life waits for no one. There are some times we miss being there for each other, but they were there praying and showing me more love then I ever seen at that time. I knew I was and am loved.

Every one of us just have our own way of showing it and to be honest, we all have our selfish moments where everything is all about us. That day was the first day I was showed that I matter and it was a long time coming. Now don't get me wrong, I always knew that my sisters loved me, but as for supporting me they never really did that over the years. I have graduated twice, held an event for my family business and no one showed up not even my mother; and I also held four more events for my business over the years and no one showed up. Needless to say, I was hurt as hell. I put my all into starting a business that I love, but I couldn't share it with the ladies I loved the most my sisters because they all had something better to do.

I kept my feelings inside about it all and anytime I could be there for one of them I was there, if I could. I will still be there because we are sisters, "I AM I MY SISTER'S KEEPER, YES I AM." I pray that we will never stop talking to each other and loving each other because I need my sisters and we need each other. It's been a long journey to get to where we are right now, and I tell you I wouldn't change anything about it. We cried, laughed, went through, and enjoyed life together at different stages in our life. So, I will just take the good with the bad and continue to thank God for all six of my sisters. There is one thing I want from my sisters just one small little big thing….

I WANT THEM ALL TO COME TO JUST ONE OF MY EVENTS. ME AND MY FAMILY PUT OUR HEART AND SOUL IN TO THIS BUSINESS AND I WOULD JUST LOVE FOR THEM TO COME ENJOY MY BLESSING WITH ME JUST ONCE…….so to all my sister's this is a request from my heart.

If I could just leave this subject with an encouraging word to someone who's relationship with their sister is not in a good place, but I would say we are sisters no matter what the situation or how deep the pain GOD can heal it. Believe some things don't happen overnight but they are worth working on. PRAY, PRAY, PRAY, AND BELIEVE IN YOUR HEART THAT GOD CAN TURN THAT THING AROUND IT. DON'T MATTER IF YOU HURT HER OR IF SHE HURT YOU GIVE IT TO GOD. ALLOW HIM TO HEAL AND STRENGTH YOU. I only tell you this because I believe I am a living testimony that GOD can take the worst of the worst and turn it around for your good.

Forgiveness

One of the most powerful acts in life is to forgive. Forgiveness will loosen you from the chains that that person has you attached to. To forgive is not just for the person you are forgiving but more so for you who has held that cancer in your soul and allowed it to eat away at you. Once you truly forgive you are free. That person no longer has chains on you and your soul will be free of cancer.

Matthew 6:14-15 King James Version (KJV)
14 For if ye forgive men their trespasses, your heavenly Father will also forgive you:
15 But if ye forgive not men their trespasses, neither will your Father forgive your trespasses.

Mark 11:25 King James Version (KJV)
25 And when ye stand praying, forgive, if ye have ought against any: that your Father also which is in heaven may forgive you your trespasses.

Colossians 3:13 King James Version (KJV)
13 Forbearing one another, and forgiving one another, if any man have a quarrel against any: even as Christ forgave you, so also [do] ye.

To all that wronged me in any way I have nothing but forgiveness and love in my heart for them. I have prayed that God would touch their heart as well as mine, and keep them in peace for I wish no harm to them and simply pray for healing and peace. I feel that to do some of the things those men did need to call for healing of the mind, because I refuse to believe that is just who they were. Maybe something happened in their life to cause them to do what they did, so I pray for healing and continue peace not just for me but for them as well. I thank God in advance for what He is about to do. I thank God for what He has already done, and I am forever grateful for this journey that in more ways than one made me who I am today.

Last words of encouragement to all my sisters out there who have experienced rape, molestation, abandonment, the loss of your child, verbal or physical abuse: please know that God is able to heal, strengthen, restore, and deliver you from whatever it is. There is nothing too big for God, and nothing is to impossible for Him to do. Know that if He can do it for me He can do it for you. I send this prayer up on today for you:

Heavenly father, I come to you with thanksgiving in my heart, humbly asking for you to touch the person/persons reading this on today. And just Lord, begin to soften their hearts and restore their faith in you, father I ask that you wrap your loving arms around their situation and cover them. Lord heal their hearts so they may forgive those who hurt them, father give them peace and the strength to move from harmful relationships, and father show them YOU. I thank you in advance for the wonderful works you are about to do in their lives, in Jesus mighty name, Amen.

Ephesians 3:20 King James Version (KJV)
[20] Now unto him that is able to do exceeding abundantly above all that we ask or think, according to the power that worketh in us,

Luke 1:37 King James Version (KJV)
[37] For with God nothing shall be impossible.

World you been served

I served you walking papers today. Your free loading riding on my joy and even working with my enemy to take me out has to go today, it was funny how you though you would win boo, but I served you your walking papers today. I rose up despite you, I stood strong and refuse to buckle from the pain you put me through. I guess the jokes on you...because today I served you your walking papers boo.

No more shackles, No more chains, No more bondage
"I AM FREE"

John 8:36 King James Version (KJV)
³⁶ If the Son therefore shall make you free, ye shall be free indeed.

Romans 8:2 King James Version (KJV)
² For the law of the Spirit of life in Christ Jesus hath made me free from the law of sin and death.

For years I was living in bondage chained down by my misguided way of life, it was as if I had 200-pound shackles on me and every step I took tore into my soul with a horrific impact on my life. In other words, I was dying. My soul was on its way to hell and my spirit was being choked out by all the toxins I had in my atmosphere. No matter how I said I wanted to live or was going to live I was killing myself slowly and painfully. Every time I allowed my flesh to decide what my spirit should have decided I died a little which caused me physical, emotional, and spiritual pain. Believe it or not, I was contemplating suicide with every wrong choice I made.

One would say I was becoming a zombie. Yes, night of the living dead type of situation. The ability to make good decision was becoming harder and harder with every passing moment. I allowed so many thoughts, memories, and pass actions to take control of my present and even my future. Yes, I spent half my life living in my pass and made it almost impossible to cope with the present situation at that time. Every time a not so comfortable situation would happen in my life one or two things would take place:

1. I would put on my make-believe I am stronger than that costume on and semi dealt with the issue at hand.

OR

2. I would automatically turn to my victim role I played so well my whole life.

Let's face it, neither one of those reactions were getting me where I needed to be and as a matter of fact, they were pushing me further from the freedom that I desired in my life. The bad relationships just got worst, the nightmares never went away, and due to me playing the chameleon role I could not get the help I needed to begin to heal so that my past would no longer control me. I was losing my mind, I had to do something, but what? At that time in my life I had become a member of Crossing Jordan Ministries, but still I wasn't being real. I was in a toxic relationship that was taking over my everything. I was addicted to weed and food and being miserable. There was no end to the trifling things I was doing, but I went to church every time the doors opened searching for a solution, a way out.

Then one day, almost a year after I joined CJM it happened right in my kitchen. The spirit of God took over, it was the scariest, wonderful, mind blowing feeling in the world. I was in my kitchen cooking while playing one of my favorite gospel CD's, Serita Versityle Campbell. I was singing and then my singing went to praying, then to thanking God, then to praising, then to worshiping God and the next thing I knew I was in full blown submission. It felt like God had just filled up my whole house and me with His spirit. I never had that experience before.

It was beyond the feeling I had at church because it was more personal like God was right there with me. That was the moment I met God and my life begin to change, freedom was coming! The process was real and had many levels, some I am still experiencing to this day. The details of my freedom are key to this book, so please allow me to walk you through what I became free from, and how the process affected every area of my life.

1. I was Freed from sexually immorality.
The first unwanted touch took place when I was thirteen and at thirty-two years old is when the last forced unwanted sexual act take place. Within those nineteen years of sexual pain I had built up a wall to keep out more pain. I became a very sexually active person; my model was if you can't beat them join them which caused me more problems within myself then any man ever did because that pain was self-afflicted. I embarked on a path that was literally killing me. The men in my life came and went. I had countless sexual partners and some I don't even

remember their name. I used my sex life as a tool to get what I wanted from men.

    Sometimes it worked and sometimes it was a bust, but no matter what I always felt disgusting after each act of sexual suicide. Over the years I became depressed, and suicidal. I couldn't tell anyone that I was now using my body as those men did when they forced themselves on me. I didn't even know why I was doing it, but I did know that I was causing so much pain in my life. I became addicted to sex, and at the same time I hated men. My whole life was a ball of confusion. I didn't know if I was straight or gay. I had to change before I killed myself which I tried about nine times already. I needed God like never before because I was at the end of my rope and it wasn't getting any better.

2. I was Freed from addictions.

With that sex addiction, I also became addicted to marijuana to dull the pain and calm my mind. Marijuana took away my ability to actually see what the sex addiction was doing to me; oh, my goodness it had me thinking I had everything under control. With every puff of that death stick I was losing all my free will. I had to stay high to be sane, I know it sounds crazy, but I was on a mind-altering substance that had me forgetting about the past pain until I needed another blunt. It was my quick fix that was taken over my life, when I came down from being high I was more confused and hurt then I was before I got high and like a deer caught in a set of headlights, I was stuck.

    I lived in a cloud, and eating so much that I could hardly stay my 235lb behind up there. Yes, food addiction came skipping right along as well, besides smoking that junk made me hungrier than a bear fresh out of hibernation. I could eat enough food for a family of four in one setting and in an hour later, go back for more. Food gave me comfort when I ate that I forgot about life for a minute, and food was like worth more than gold in my book. I ate if I was happy, mad, or sad it didn't matter the occasion I ate. That addiction was so strong it too took over me. It didn't matter if I smoked or not I ate, snacking was my friend and I didn't need no one as long as I had food. Food normally came as a pick me up for whatever situation that was bothering me at that moment.

3. I was freed from family hurt.
The relationships I had with my family contributed a lot to my addictions. Most people had their mother and father's side of the family, but I had my mother's side, my father side's and my adopted family mother's side of the family to deal with and each side came with enough pain to drive a very sane person insane. In between all three sides of my family I dealt with abandonment, molestation, neglect, favoritism, and addiction. Family hurt was the worst, these were the people that were entrusted with my young life to shape and mold me into a productive citizen in society. They were also supposed to protect me from things that they put me through, but I learned firsthand from my family how it feels to not be protected but subjected to the sick things of this world right in the places where I called home. I see firsthand that I just didn't matter to no one, which gave me no good excuse to do the things I did, but it was the reason why I did those things. I needed to hide all the past hurt.

3. I was Freed from shame.
And by hiding the past hurt I created a whole wall of shame for myself that I had to look at every day. I used to have flash backs that knocked me to my knees, it was like watching someone else do those horrible acts of sex, and violence. I used my addictions to cover up my shame, so all everyone saw was a fun loving, caring, helping, love to cook Charlotte. Feeding people was one of my clean addictions because it covered my shame perfectly. When people were enjoying my food and service they didn't see or pay attention to my sex problem, or my weight problem, or my smoking habit which also included cigarettes.

They didn't see the hate I had built up for men, or clinginess I had toward woman of power in my eyes. They didn't catch that I may have looked like an adult but I had a childlike mind, and at times became confused in adult conversations which I also learned how to cover up with humor. It's funny how one thing led to another and one issue created an even bigger issue, but I found out THERE IS NOTHING IMPOSSIBLE FOR GOD!!! He begins to release those shackles and break those chains and erase that bondage that I was in. Every time I took one step toward God chains begin to fall off. The more I learned the more empowered I became.

Reading the bible was like having the best motivational speaker ever in the palm of your hands and you could hear Him whenever you wanted to. All you had to do was open His book. God begin to reveal things in my life to me and confirm some decisions I made were led by Him. It was like a breath of fresh air to finally feel some of the weigh from years fall off. Tears of joy started to replace tears of shame and despair. My worship was beginning to truly be worship not just a blank verbal petition to, please make my life better. I learned how to thank God for just being Him and loving me even though I was filled with flaws. Every day was a new chance to build a closer relationship with Him and I was taking full advantage of it.

I Changed

My walk is not the same Lord
I Changed
Family and friends notice I'm no longer lit Lord
I changed
The darkness I was living has now turned to light Lord
I changed
My path is not traveled by most, but I love that you Lord is my host,
yes
Lord I changed
I have nothing but thanks in my soul, for with love and joy my cup over flows due to the sudden but so welcome Changed in my world oh yes, Lord your child Has Changed

In 2013, I was newly divorced. Finally, freed from that toxic relationship that was sucking me dry and I was ready to find myself again. I had been on my walk with God for eight years at that point, and it was full of falls that almost take me out, but my God never gave up on me. I was now at the end of my rope and I had no more times to mess up. I needed to start living a life that represented Jesus. God was still working on my many flaws and sometimes I would step out of His way and let Him work, but other times when I thought I was helping I was in the way and seriously at risk of losing it all. Thank God He knew my heart and my desire to please Him in spite of my falls, so He gave me another chance.

One day my friend from church who's she like a little sister to me, was having one of our many conversations on relationship and marriage, and we decided to pray to God together and ask Him to send us our Boaz. We both were specific about what we asked for in a mate. I believe it was around early April or May, I prayed to God and asked Him to send me to a God-fearing family man who worked and knew how to take care of home and his family. Someone who didn't want anything to do with the street life and someone I could be in ministry with.

Philippians 4:6 King James Version (KJV)
[6] Be careful for nothing; but in every thing by prayer and supplication with thanksgiving let your requests be made known unto God.

Matthew 7:7-8 King James Version (KJV)
[7] Ask, and it shall be given you; seek, and ye shall find; knock, and it shall be opened unto you:
[8] For every one that asketh receiveth; and he that seeketh findeth; and to him that knocketh it shall be opened.

To be honest, I asked God for a husband that was nothing like me, but who I wanted to be and needed to be to achieve a closer relationship with God. As long as I was single I risked the chance of sinning sexually. That's how I seen myself and I didn't want to disappoint God, so I put my head in the holy book and stayed in prayer. My falls seem to become a few and the only thing I considered against God was that I was looking for a friend only because I spent too much time talking to men and not enough talking to God. Until that day arrived, the day I met my husband. It was just a normal day and I was waiting on the bus stop.

He asked me with a huge smile, "do you have the time?"

I looked on my phone and told him the time, it seems like we connected somehow that day without saying another word to each other. I thought about him after that day and could not get him off my mind it was unreal. He was not the type of man I was attracted to, not at all. I wanted an educated thug with a New York/ California swag who loved God. I wanted a dressed up, clean cut gangster of love type of dude who checked off all the emotional and spiritual characteristic on my list I gave God in my prayer, but this cat was different. He was a little scruffy, kind of rough around the edges but he had a look of hard work written all over his face with a smile that could charm a woman out of whatever he wanted. In a good way.

We actually met in passing two more times before we got up the nerves to exchange numbers. It was June of 2013, we seen each other on the #15 bus and I gave him my number as I got off on my stop. Something in me felt so funny like I had butterflies in my stomach. I got in the house, throw my phone on the sofa and ran to the bathroom. When I came out of the bathroom my daughter was yelling, "Lawrence is on the phone."

After I explained to the kiddy patrol who he was I answered the call to the rest of my life. We talked until he went to work, and then we texted. Him and I, never stopped talking from that day forward, we tried a few times, but it didn't work because we'd always end up calling or texting each other. It was like we were two love sick teenagers. During that time, we found out that our churches fellowshipped with each other, we stayed down the street from each other, our birthdays were one day away from each other, we were the same age, and that our lives have crossed paths many times within the last four or five years. It was like being in the twilight zone.

I am going with one of his favorite verses…

Proverbs 18:22 King James Version (KJV)
[22] Whoso findeth a wife findeth a good thing, and obtaineth favour of the LORD.

He proposed to me and we were married December 7, 2013 and my life has changed forever. God answered my prayer and believe me when I say much is giving much is required. With the start of my new marriage, I was blessed with someone who helped me and is still helping me pray and stay in the word. Although my change came at a cost, it was well worth it. God had freed me from sexually immorality, addictions, family hurt, and shame. My life was finally showing fruit of my labor. I could see the light for real this time and it was clear as the stars in the sky under a perfect moonlight. It was calling me to embrace the change, and love the new me while enjoying the peace, for in His mist all was well. The beginning of my freedom sprung up like a new bud after it died and turned into a beautiful flower.

The turn up is real. I have been lit by the king and my party will never end with my hands in the air and my eyes opened wide I praise the one and only God. The turn up is on fire, it takes me higher and higher just to serve a God who has me lit and dancing with peace that comes straight from above while he shows me true unconditional love. The turn up is everlasting, now I'm truly on one reaping all the benefits of my praying and fasting ... I turn up even more knowing that my turn up for God is win, win, win and all gain, and his blessing right on time will remain the same.

The new Charlotte was a long time coming. I never imagine feeling this good about being me. I never again will compromise who I am in the Lord to please anyone else, this flesh has been serve notice that my walk is real and my relationship with the KING is tight. I am more focus on pleasing God now, so what if I don't fit in I bet I won't force it. I am on a killing spree murdering this flesh daily with the word.

Romans 12:2 King James Version (KJV)
² And be not conformed to this world: but be ye transformed by the renewing of your mind, that ye may prove what is that good, and acceptable, and perfect, will of God.

I recently was put in a situation where I learned that I am changed. I am happy to say my oldest sister is getting married and she asked me to be the matron of honor, of course I said yes. That was so important to me. Not only do I get to be there but to take such an important part in her wedding is awesome. In between time, I had two strokes and was out of work etc., but my father stepped in and helped my husband and I so we could still be in her wedding. So, at the dress fitting I was so excited I could get everyone together so I could plan the best bridal shower/bachelorette party ever. I had to pay for my dress and while I was doing that my sister all loud and rudely let it be known she didn't want me to do it because I don't live like they do.

    She took away another chance for me to show her what my business was really about. My husband and I have a catering/event planning business, I know this is her wedding but I was just a little hurt about it all to tell you the truth. One good thing did come out of that day she ripped my heart out and fed it to me. I realized that I have changed. I often asked God if I was really saved because I didn't see a change in me, but it became clear to me that I wasn't looking through my spiritual eye or I would have seen all I gave up living saved.

    I spent too much time focusing on what I was doing wrong to see if I CHANGED…. Everyone else who knew me saw the change in me, but after I cried about not being accepted and complained about it, God showed me that I was being a fool. I shouldn't be crying but rejoicing for there will come a time when my business will be well received, this was just not the time. This was just to show me what I have been asking for years. Growth comes in many shapes and forms, and brings some hurt and joy from letting some things go, but if we don't accept the change because you're too busy looking at other people's change thinking you are supposed to change like them, then we all will miss our own moment. I did for years but thank God He waited for me to see it for myself.

    There are no more shackles, chains, or bondage holding me down I can move and I can breathe. No longer bounded by the thirty-five years of pain and heartache I carried with me. What you see now is truly what you get. I put up my chameleon costume, as a matter of fact I burnt it and give it up to God as a burnt offering. This here chic is free; hate me or love me I AM FREE! Ride with me or not I AM FREE! To be able to forgive all the men who laid their unwanted hands on me is FREEDOM. To walk in love, peace, and joy after living through hell, now that's FREEDOM. To be able to show my own children what being healed and set free looks like, that's FREEDOM.

    To finally be in a marriage where I am loved and respected for who I am that truly is FREEDOM. FREEDOM came at a price that I could not pay. It was heavy on my heart, mind, body, soul, and spirit, but I didn't have to do it alone. I was carried some of the way, the cost was cut down too little or nothing at times, and I was covered from mostly all of it before I gave God my life. Before I knew Him, He did that for me because He knew one day I would submit to Him; so, He waited. Such a powerful act by my God almighty, bread of life, the bright morning star, the holy one, the way maker, healer, Yahweh. Yet He waited on me who is not worthy of all his mercy. I am forever humbled and grateful for my life crazy as it may sound, but I am. My life has molded me into the woman that I am today. It pushed me closer to the one and only true God, my savior who restored me, saved me, cleaned me up, and provided me with a way to keep going on.

Freedom

To me means that I am………
Freed from my past
Revived for my future
Established through the Word
Exalted by GOD
Delivered from unforgiveness and hate
Overjoyed by GOD's grace and
Mercy over my life

The fourth turning point

The last turning point in my life was the year 2013, when I started a new marriage. Now I know as long as I am in the land of the living more turning points will come, but this one right here marks a new beginning in my life. Not just with my husband, but with God. I started to grow into the woman God has created me to be, walking in true love, and forgiveness; submitting to God with my life. I want to say the end, but it's not. This story will continue to go on until God calls me home, so I will just say until next time I bid you all love, peace, and thanks….

Remember to always be thankful for your past no matter how it was. It helped you become who you are today. The good times loved you, the hard times made you strong, and the in between times kept you balanced, so now you can take on the world. Much love, blessings, and peace to you all and just like a pastor I will once again say my closing……lol. Laughing is good for your soul….

Acknowledgments

I would like to first give thanks to God, who is the head of my life, the captain of my sea, and my way maker. This would not be possible without His love that covered me through the years. To my awesome husband Lawrence Shand, I thank you for understanding the healing that this project brought to me and for your love, encouragement, and support. To my wonderful daughter and son, DeAnna and DaBreon who stood by me pushing me and encouraging me to complete this book, I truly thank you and love you so much for your support. To our other beautiful babies Devin, Daja, Shelda, Alexander, and Nathanael and our bonus child Tifarah, I love you all and I am blessed to be your mom, thank you for being part of my journey. I also give thanks to Regina Fletcher, my ride or die cousin for always being there for me. You always encouraged me and believed in me even when I didn't believe in myself, thank you girl for being a true friend. To my Crossing Jordan Family, I am so grateful that I have you all in my life, thank you Pastors' Rodney and Serita Campbell for leading and guiding me to God over the 14 plus years that I have been a member of CJM. Thank you, Minster Rosezina Campbell for your love and support, you are a blessing to me and I thank God for putting you in my life.

Special Thanks

I must give thanks to my mother Arnell Jefferson, even in death you have a great impact on my life and I thank you for being the best mother while you were here. I love you and miss you everyday mom.

To my dad Jimmie Gray, my super hero. I love you with my whole heart, your life has not been easy, but I never saw you give up. You have played a huge part in my life and it's because of you I refuse to give up no matter what. Love you

And to my mom Shelda McCorty, my angel. To try to put it in words how I feel about you would be too much, so I will say this thank you for being my mom. It's said that you only get one mom, but you proved that saying wrong when you took me in and loved and cared for me like I was your own. Mom, I do not know where I would have been if you wouldn't have, so selflessly took on the huge task of loving me. I thank God so much for you.

And to my siblings Shannon, Lateasha, Enetrea, Shawneen, Ya'nique, Loreena, Jimmie Jr, Toran and Lemar… I love you all. We may not have been on the same page at times in our lives, but the love we have for each other has helped me grow. In between all the arguing, fussing, fighting there was so much love and I am blessed to have you all in my life.

"Where the writers go…"
www.sycwp.com
home4writers@sycwp.com

www.ingramcontent.com/pod-product-compliance
Lightning Source LLC
Chambersburg PA
CBHW071006160426
43193CB00012B/1946